MW01488376

The Kurdish Question and Turkish-Iranian Relations

From World War I to 1998

Kurdish Studies Series
Number 1

The Kurdish Question
and
Turkish-Iranian Relations

From World War I to 1998

Robert Olson

Mazda Publishers
1998

Mazda Publishers
Academic Publishers Since 1980
P.O. Box 2603
Costa Mesa, California 92626 U.S.A.
www.mazdapub.com

Library of Congress Cataloging-in-Publication Data
Olson, Robert W.
The Kurdish Question and Turkish-Iranian Relations:
From World War I to 1998/ Robert Olson
p.cm.—(Kurdish Studies Series; No 1)
Includes bibliographical references and index.

ISBN:1-56859-067-9
(cloth:alk. paper)

1. Kurds—Turkey—Politics and government. 2. Kurds—Iran—Politics and
government. 3. Turkey—foreign relations—Iran. 4. Iran—foreign relations—
Turkey. 5. Turkey—Ethnic relations. 6. Iran—Ethnic relations.
I. Title. II. Series.
DR435.k87045 1998
327.561055—dc21
98-9898
CIP

To the Kurdish peoples: may they live
when their existence is no longer
defined as a 'question' or
a 'problem'

CONTENTS

Acknowledgments

I wish to thank my colleagues Kristin Stapleton, Dan Rowland, Bruce Eastwood and David Olster for agreeing to read this manuscript in draft at the busy beginning of fall semester. Kristin was especially gracious. Only the foolhardy or interested would have done so. I am especially grateful to Angelique Galskis for her acute eye and sharp pencil. I am deeply appreciative. My two walking buddies, Art Wrobel and John Cawelti, proved that they can out-proof-read as well as out-pace me. I relish their abilities and their willingness to listen to my babble as we walk. I wish to thank Nader Entessar for gracious giving of time and for his comments. I hope that Dr. Ahmad Jabbari will be rewarded for inviting me to write this inaugural essay for the new *Kurdish Studies Series* that he is initiating at Mazda Publishers. I also want to remind Judith that I love her very much.

Note on Spelling and Names

I have followed, for the most part, modern Turkish spelling as it renders correctly the pronunciation of Turkish and Kurdish names. This makes the pronunciation of Turkish and Kurdish names more understandable not only to the English reader but also to the Turkish and Kurdish readers. In modern Turkish, the letters *ö* and *ü* are similar to the German letters. The letter *i* is pronounced as it is in *sit* in English. There is also an undotted *ı* in Turkish, which sounds like the *u* in *stadium*. The letters *ç* and *ş* are similar to the *ch* in *church* and the *sh* in *should*. The *c* is pronounced like the *j* in *John*. Turkish also has a letter *ğ* which has the effect of lengthening the preceding vowel and sometimes obviates the need to pronounce the following consonants, as in *ağa* (large landowner). I have spelled certain words such as Azerbaijan as it is normally spelled in English. I have spelled Sinjan using the English *j* rather than the Turkish *c* in order to render it closer to its actual pronunciation in English. For the Farsi names and spellings I have relied on the system used by the *Ettela'at* and *Tehran Times* newspapers which I used in my research.

English Translations of Political Parties and Organizations

Translations	English	Turkish
Democracy Party	DP	DEP
Democratic Party	DP	DEP
Kurdistan Democratic Party	KDP	KDP
Kurdistan Democratic Party of Iran	KDPI	KDPI
Kurdistan Workers' Party	KWP	PKK
Motherland Party	MP.	ANAP
National Salvation Party	NSP	MSP
Patriotic Union of Kurdistan	PUK	KYP
Peoples Democracy Party	PDP	HADEP
Peoples Labor Party	PLP	HEP
Republican Peoples Party	RPP	CHP
Social Democratic Party	SDP	SHP
Socialist Party of Turkey-Kurdistan	TSKP	SKP-T
Kurdistan Socialst Party	KSP	KSP
True Path Party	TPP	DYP
Welfare Party	WP	RP

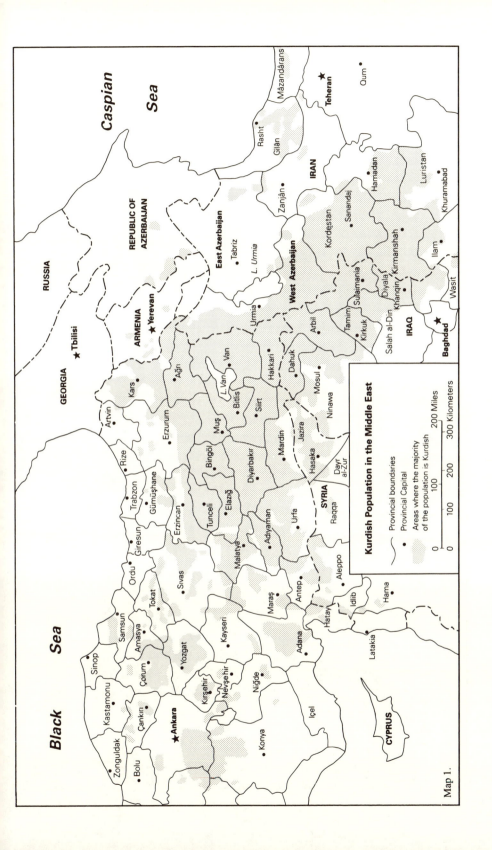

Map 1.

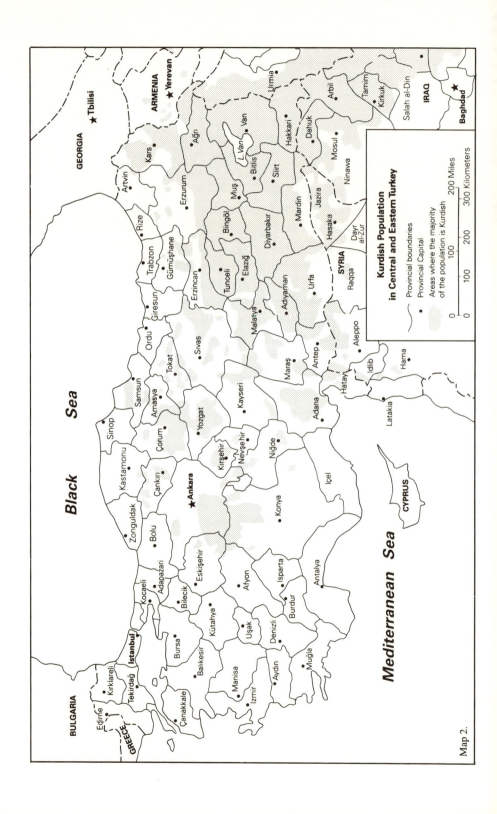

Kurdish Population in Central and Eastern Turkey

— Provincial boundaries

• Provincial Capital

Areas where the majority of the population is Kurdish

0   100   200 Miles

0 100 200 300 Kilometers

Black Sea

Mediterranean Sea

BULGARIA

GREECE

Edirne

Kırklareli

Tekirdağ

İstanbul

Çanakkale

Kocaeli

Adapazarı

Bilecik

Bursa

Balıkesir

Manisa

İzmir

Aydın

Kütahya

Uşak

Denizli

Muğla

Eskişehir

Afyon

Isparta

Burdur

Antalya

Zonguldak

Bolu

Çankırı

Ankara

Kırşehir

Nevşehir

Niğde

Konya

İçel

Kastamonu

Sinop

Çorum

Yozgat

Kayseri

Samsun

Amasya

Tokat

Sivas

Ordu

Giresun

Rize

Trabzon

Gümüşhane

Erzincan

Tunceli

Elazığ

Malatya

Adıyaman

Maraş

Antep

Hatay

Adana

Latakia

CYPRUS

Artvin

Erzurum

Ağrı

Kars

Muş

Bingöl

Diyarbakır

Urfa

L.Van

Van

Bitlis

Siirt

Mardin

Jazira

Hasaka

Hakkari

Dahuk

Ninawa

Mosul

Arbil

Tamim

Kirkuk

Salah al-Din

Urmia

SYRIA

Raqqa

Dayr al-Zur

Aleppo

Idlib

Hama

GEORGIA

Tbilisi

ARMENIA

Yerevan

IRAQ

Baghdad

Map 2.

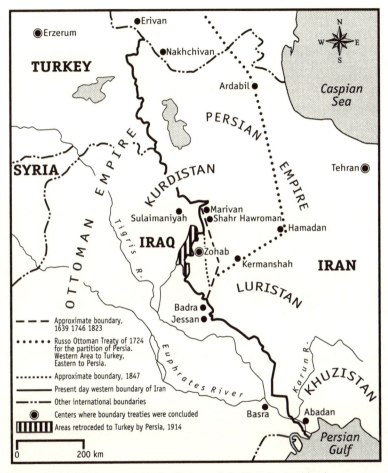

Map 3. Territorial changes along the Ottoman, Safavid, Qajan land borders, 1639-1914.

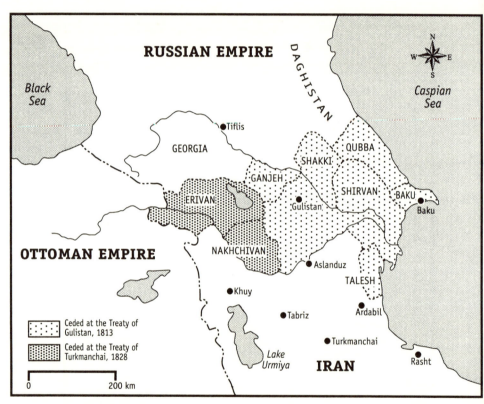

Map 4. Iran's territorial losses in the Caucasus from 1813-1828.

Preface

I am pleased to offer this essay as the inaugural volume of the new *Kurdish Studies Series* to be published by Mazda Publishers. Dr. Ahmad Jabbari, publisher of the Press, is determined that this series will make available the newest and best work published on the history, politics and culture of the Kurds.

It is about time. The history of the Kurds and the significant role they have played in Middle East and Islamic history is the most neglected area of research and publication in Middle East and Islamic studies. One reason for this is that the field of Middle East and Islamic studies has long been dominated by scholars and people interested in Arab, Turkish or Iranian history. Indeed, more has been published in the last twenty-five years on the history of the Jews in the Middle East than on the entire history of the Kurds. Middle East and Islamic studies also have been dominated by Europeans and Americans interested in Arab, Turkish and Iranian history and cultures or scholars from those lands.

There are other reasons for the lack of Kurdish studies. Such studies, as is implicit in the following essay, would have served the interests of the imperial Great Powers, especially the interests of Great Britain. For this reason it is most appropriate that the inaugural volume in the *Kurdish Studies Series* begin with a study of the Kurdish question in its geopolitical and geostrategical context over the past five centuries and especially during the last two decades.

The following essay concentrates on the Kurdish question— i.e., the challenge of the Kurds and of Kurdish nationalism in the interstate relations of Turkey and Iran. There are several reasons for this selection. The few scholarly studies that do exist concerning the Kurds have generally been confined to the Kurds in Iraq. This is because, as the *Introduction* makes clear, Great Britain's control of the Middle East in the post-WW I era depended on its control of Iraq in which the Kurds were major players. There is no question that the historical and political impact of the Kurds on Iraq is immense. The results of the 1991 Persian Gulf war are proof of this. But the consequences of the Persian Gulf war have emphasized again the pivotal role that Turkey and Iran played, continue to play and the great interest that they have in containing the challenge of Kurdish nationalism referred to euphemistically as the "Kurdish Problem" in its intrastate dimensions and as the "Kurdish Question" in its trans-state context.

What I try to do in the following essay is to extract the essential facts of the Kurdish question and the Kurdish problems that affect directly Turkey's and Iran's internal and external policies.

Both Turkey and Iran have Kurdish problems. The substantial Kurdish population is in itself a major factor. The Kurdish population of Turkey is approximately 12 to 14 million, representing 18 to 21 percent of the a total population of some 65 million. Turkey's Kurdish problem and its intermingling with the Kurdish question has dominated Turkish politics for over a decade. Just a few statistics demonstrate its significance. Turkey has had some 400,000 military personnel in eastern and southeastern Turkey during the last decade. The cost of its war against the PKK and its suppression of other Kurds was estimated to cost around $10 billion per year by 1997. This figure does not include an approximate cost of another 3 to 4 billion in other sectors of the economy. Three thousand six hundred villages and hamlets have been destroyed. Over 300 journalists, mostly Kurdish, have been murdered. There were 3,000 other "unsolved" killings. But by far the most drastic consequence of Ankara's war and ethnic cleansing practices against the PKK and Kurds, in order to deprive the PKK of a sympathetic environment, has been the flight of some 3 million Kurds to the larger cities within the east and southeast and to the large cities in the West, especially Ankara, Istanbul and Izmir. The migration has been so monumental that some cities and towns along the Mediterranean that twenty years ago had no Kurds now have populations that are half Kurdish.

The Kurdish problem—or as the Turks say, "reality," although there is very little realization on their part—is so pressing that the Turkish government and censorship bureau have recently allowed a Turkish scholar, Kemal Kirişci, and a British colleague, Gareth Winrow, to publish *The Kurdish Question in Turkey: An Example of a Trans-State Ethnic Conflict* . This is the first book published in English to deal seriously and in a scholarly way with the great challenge posed to the Turkish state by the Kurds: the greatest since the creation of the republic in 1923. It seems unlikely, however, that the present Turkish government or any Turkish government will heed some of the solutions proffered by the authors. The reason for this pessimistic view is that Kirişci and Winrow do not address the wider geopolitical and geostrategical context that compels the Turkish state to continue its war against the PKK and the Kurds and the ethnic cleansing, especially along the Iraq and Syria borders, that accompany it. The following essay attempts to provide that geopolitical and geostrategical context.

The difficulties of Turkish scholars in writing scholarly articles about Turkey's Kurdish challenge is well illustrated by Metin Heper, the Dean of the College of Administrative and Social Sciences at Bilkent University, the premier university in Turkey. Heper is perhaps the best known Turkish political scientist. Writing in the *Armed Forces Journal* (vol. 22, no. 4 [1996]:638) regarding the military and democracy in Turkey, Heper concluded "...sure of its continuing high status in the Turkish polity and society, thanks to its avoidance of involvement in day-to-day politics, the Turkish military can afford to forego most of its powers and prerogatives." One year later, writing in *The Middle East Journal* (vol. 51, no. 1 [1997]:45) on the topic of Islam and Democracy in Turkey, Heper concluded that "A marriage between Islam and democracy can be consummated if the radical secularists stop trying to impose their preferred life-style and set of values upon the Islamists, and if the latter do not attempt to undermine by word or deed the basic tenets of the secular democratic state in Turkey." Yet, less than six months after Heper published this article, the military toppled the government of Necmettin Erbakan. The Turkish Armed Forces (TAF) commanders justified their action by proclaiming that "reactionism," i.e., the Islamist movement, was a threat to the state. This demonstrates how far off the mark recent analyses of Turkish politics have been. I hope that my essay will correct some of these misplaced prognosticians.

Iran's Kurdish problem presents less of a threat to the configuration of the Iranian government and state than in Turkey. But the difference is one of degree. The Kurdish population of Iran is estimated to be around 6 million or about 10 percent out of a total population of 60 million. The Kurdish nationalist challenge in Iran during the twentieth century has not been as great as that in Turkey, in spite of the fact that the first and only independent Kurdish state ever to be established was in Iran from 1945 to 1946. But the creation of the Kurdish Mahabad Republic, although an authentic expression of Kurdish nationalism and will, was also a consequence of the politics of the later years of WW II and the emergent vicissitudes of Cold War politics. After the Islamic revolution in Iran, the new Iranian government had the advantage of attempting to contain Kurdish nationalism by emphasizing an inclusive Islamic ideological discourse. Turkey did not have this instrumental advantage. After the military came to power in 1980, the generals tried to use such a discourse against the leftist challenge, but, rather than diminishing Kurdish nationalism, it increased it.

Iran's great concern with regard to its Kurdish problem is that Ankara's dissatisfaction with its efforts to cooperate in controlling the PKK will impel Turkey to encourage Turkish nationalism among its Azeri population, estimated to be around 10 million or 16.5 percent of a total population of 60 million. As far as Tehran is concerned, the Kurdish question is intimately tied to the Azeri question.

One of the most interesting aspects of scholarly studies dealing with Iran's foreign policy is that they pay scant attention to that country's relations with Turkey. It is as though scholars dealing with the topic of Iran's foreign relations are mesmerized by Tehran's relations with the West, especially the United States, and with security studies on the Perisan Gulf. This tendency is exhibited in two of the best recent studies on Iran's foreign policy during the last decade. K. L. Afrasiabi's, *After Khomeini: New Directions in Iran's Foreign Policy* barely mentions Iran's relations with Turkey or the Kurds. The words Kurdistan or Kurds appear only eight times in the index. The second study, Anoushiravan Ehteshami's *After Khomeini: The Second Iranian Republic* provides a bit more coverage on the subject, but he, too, has only two citations on the Kurds and they are in reference to the Kurdish Democratic Party (KDP). My aim in the following essay to correct these omissions.

The significance of the two countries' Kurdish problems, which in Turkey is crucial to the survival of the state in its present configuration, compels them to try to manage the problems via the trans-state Kurdish question and by cooperating on their shared wider geopolitical and geostrategical interests. Regimes—and in the case of Turkey, state survival—depend on such management. This is the topic of the following essay.

Robert Olson
University of Kentucky
December, 1997

The Kurdish Question and
Turkish-Iranian Relations
From World War I to 1998

Introduction

Or Why Was No Kurdish State Created After WW I?

The Kurds are a people estimated to number some 20-25 million living largely in four Middle East countries: Turkey with some 12-14 million; Iran with 6 million; Iraq, 3.5-4 million and, Syria with 1 million. In addition, approximately 100-150,000 Kurds live in Armenia and Azerbaijan. Recent reports suggest there may be between 300,000 and 1 million Kurds living within the Russian Federation. Since the bulk of Kurds live in contiguous areas of east and southeast Turkey; north and northeast Iraq; north and northwest Iran and in northeastern Syria, they have possessed a sense of self, community and shared space since medieval times at least. This sense of identity was reinforced by the emergence of large rebellions in the last quarter of the nineteenth century that strengthened further their sense of community.

The Kurds consider themselves to be direct descendants of the ancient Medes (although modern scholarship doubts this) who, because of military conquests, defeats and collapse of empires, began to migrate and locate themselves around 2,000 years ago in the mountain fastnesses of the present day states of Turkey, Iran, Iraq and Syria. From these strategic and almost impregnable locations, the Kurds were able to preserve their communities while at the same time participating in the great Armenian, Greek, Byzantine, Arab, Turkish, Safavid, Qajar and Ottoman empires that dominated this region's history right up to the collapse of the Ottoman and Qajar empires at the end of WW I. The Kurds were promised the possibility of an independent state in Articles 62 and 64 of the Treaty of Sèvres signed on 10 August 1920.

The geopolitics of the Middle East after the Persian Gulf war in 1991 seemed to suggest that the possibility of the creation of a Kurdish state existed for the first time since WW I, with the nucleus of that state to be established in northern Iraq, the very area which the British empire had incorporated into the Iraqi state between 1918 and 1926. The circumstances as to why a Kurdish state was not created in the 1920s resembles the situation of the 1990s when, again, the geopolitical circumstances did not allow for the establishment of a Kurdish state. This is the subject of the following essay. But because of the similarity between the geopolitical circumstances of the 1920 and 1990s, we must ask the question as to why the European powers, especially Great Britain, entertained the idea of a Kurdish state in the first place after WW I.

The major reason favoring the creation of a Kurdish state after WW I was the concern of the European powers to place a buffer between the Turks of Anatolia and the Turkic speaking peoples of Central Asia in the Caucasus, and especially in Azerbaijan. It is important to note that the vast majority of Anatolian Turks and Central Asian Turks are Sunnis. It is true that almost all Azerbaijanis are Shi'i but, with this one exception, the Sunni belt stretches from Istanbul to Beshkek (formerly Frunze), the capital of Krygystan. Given the potential of Muslim unity, although subsequently realized to be exaggerated, Britain, the dominant and, in many instances, ruling power in the region, was eager to prevent any such unity from taking place.

A second reason for the creation of a Kurdistan was to create a buffer state between emergent nationalist Turkey and the autonomous republic of Azerbaijan in the Soviet Union. A third reason was to create a buffer between Turkey and the Azeri population of Iran. The vast majority of Kurds are Sunni. The Sunniness of a Kurdish state would distinguish it from the Shi'iness of both Azerbaijans. A Kurdish state would have another geostrategical advantage as far as Britain and other European states were concerned: it would reduce the potential power of Turkey, Iran and Iraq. A Kurdish state that encompassed what Kurdish nationalists considered the Kurdish regions of eastern and southeastern Turkey would have deprived the new republic of significant portions of its claimed territory and substantially reduced access to transportation routes to the Caucasus, Iran and Iraq and Syria. Indeed, it would have placed a virtual buffer between Turks and Arabs. Much of the water resources and potential hydroelectric and irrigation systems would have been in or near the Kurdish state. The creation of a Kurdish state would have allowed any of the contiguous states as well as the Soviet Union and European powers, especially Britain or France, to utilize the Kurdish state and the Kurdish population against Turkey or Iran. During the Kurdish rebellions against Turkey in 1925 and 1930, the Turkish government and media frequently accused Britain and the Soviet Union of abetting the rebels. During the Kurdish Ararat rebellion in the 1930s, Turkey accused Iran of aiding the insurgents.

A Kurdish state, even one confined to territory in northern Iraq, could have proven advantageous in intimidating the new nationalist states of

Turkey and Iran. Although Britain decided finally not to create a Kurdish state in its mandated territory of Iraq, it continued to encourage moderate Kurdish nationalism in Iraq, both as an instrument to establish a balance of power between the Kurds and the Arabs, both Sunnis and Shi'is, to control Iraq and, in turn, to utilize Iraq as the major instrument to implement its Sharifian policy, i.e., to use the Sunni-Arab Hashemite dynasty as collaborators in controlling the eastern Arab lands. No evidence has emerged to show that Britain supported Kurdish nationalist movements within Turkey or Iran after 1923. Encouraging militant Kurdish nationalism would have threatened British control, but by encouraging moderate Kurdish nationalism, Britain was able to compel the Kurds of Iraq to accept or at least acquiesce in, British policies toward the Arab countries. The acquiescent policies of the Kurds of Iraq toward the British after 1923 bear striking similarities to the policies they pursued toward the United States after the Persian Gulf war in 1991.

As long as Great Britain was in control of Iraq, it encouraged moderate or bland Kurdish nationalism. The Kurds of Iraq fulfilled the same geopolitical and geostrategical purposes as a Kurdish state might have as far as British objectives toward Turkey and Iran were concerned. The threat of Kurdish nationalism emanating from British controlled Iraq proved an effective instrument in compelling Turkey and Iran to concentrate on domestic issues and in preventing them from meddling in other countries' affairs. The threat of Kurdish nationalism also prevented Turkey and Iran from taking strong actions in the affairs of the Arab countries, all under British and French control. This was especially true in the case of Iraq. In fact, it is probable that the threat of Kurdish nationalism contributed to Kemal Ataturk's dictum: "Peace at home and peace abroad." This is a motto that the Turkish government continued to announce officially up to the 1990s. Ironically, it was the Persian Gulf war and resurgence of Kurdish nationalism in northern Iraq and in Turkey itself that led the government to renounce Ataturk's dictum.

While the Kurdish nationalist movement in Iran during the inter-war period was weaker than Turkey's, the threat of Kurdish nationalism had a similar effect of containing a more adventurous Iranian foreign policy. Such a policy would have allowed the British to respond with the cudgel of stirring up the Kurds in Iran. One of the reasons for the good relations between Turkey and the Soviet Union, in addition to the help that the Bolsheviks gave to the Kemalists during and after their war of independence, was Turkey's desire to prevent the Bosheviks from meddling with or encouraging Kurdish nationalism. Preventing Soviet support for Kurdish nationalism became a priority of Turkish foreign policy, especially after Turkey adopted a more pronounced Western oriented foreign policy in the late 1920s and 1930s. The "Kurdish card" remained a persistent factor in relations between Russia and Turkey after the collapse of the Soviet Union. Moscow gave political and military support to the PKK as long as Ankara supported and provided military and financial aid to the Chechens in their war against Russia in the early 1990s. Before the Chechen defeat of the Russians in 1996, the Kurdish question was a major factor in Turkish-Russian relations.

It is important to stress, however, with regard to Iraq, that Britain also cooperated with Iran in suppressing and killing the most ardent of the Kurdish nationalists. A strong Kurdish nationalist movement in Iran would have directly impacted British policies in Iraq. The British also used policing and bombing raids to quash Kurdish resistance. By 1932, most of the Kurdish nationalist leaders had been eliminated and their movements and followers were brought under British and Iraqi control. Shaykhs Taha, Mahmud and Simko Agha, some of the most famous Kurdish leaders, were removed from power, and in the case of Simko killed, in this case by the Iranian army. The Iranians acted against Simko Agha because they knew that to do so correlated with British policy. During the inter-war period the governments of Turkey, Iran and British-controlled Iraq had national security agreements that they would not encourage Kurdish nationalism in each other's countries. This meant that Turkey and Iran pursued policies to suppress Kurdish nationalism and that Britain, for its own reasons, chose to encourage Kurdish nationalism in Iraq, albeit a nationalist one of the blandest type possible.

There are other reasons why Britain did not support a Kurdish independent state in the northern portion of Iraq mandated to its control. Almost all of these reasons had to do with Britain's geopolitical schemes for the Arab countries of the central Middle East. By the time Faysal assumed the throne in August 1921, it was clear that the Sharifian family was to be crucial to evolving British policy in Iraq and for the Middle East, excluding Syria and Lebanon, where the French were ensconced. It was necessary after 1921 for the British to secure the throne for King Faysal in order to strengthen its Sharifian policy in Jordan and the Hejaz. Iraq was the pivot of this policy. There were many obstacles to the consolidation of British power in Iraq, but one of the most pressing was the difficulties of determining the Turkish-Iraqi border. The Lausanne Treaty (24 July 1923) had not resolved the Mosul question and as a result boundaries were not determined. It was left to the Anglo-Iraq and Turkey

Treaty of 5 June 1926 to establish the boundary between Iraq and Turkey. The boundary accepted by all parties in 1926 still obtains in spite of the threats of the Turkish government after 1992 to move the boundary 10 to 15 miles southward in order to counter the attacks that the PKK was launching against Turkish targets from that area.

In order to consolidate its position in Iraq after putting Faysal in power in 1921, Great Britain had to establish or support a Kurdish state whether beyond or within the borders of Iraq. But the success of the Turkish nationalist forces ended the possibility of the creation of a Kurdish state in territories that the new republic of Turkey claimed after 1923. The new Turkish republic did not recognize any Kurdish claims in its newly declared territories. Once it was decided in late 1921 that Iraq was to be pivotal to the sharifian policy for British control of the Middle East, it was necessary for Britain to abandon the idea of a Kurdish state outside of its mandate in Iraq. The principle reason for this change was that the British determined that the Kurds of Iraq were crucial to ensure their consolidation of power in Iraq which was pivotal to their domination of the Middle East. In addition the oil fields around Kirkuk were in and near heavily populated Kurdish areas.

The Sunni Kurds, especially their leadership, both religious and secular, were a necessary balance to the Shi'i Arabs. Indeed, King Faysal, as a representative of the Sunnis, was even more apprehensive than the British regarding the potential power of the Shi'is. Faysal stated his fears to Sir Percy Cox, British High Commissioner in Iraq, a few months after assuming the throne. Faysal told Cox that

> The question of Kurdistan had further aspect for him as king of Iraq which had probably not been fully considered by us [British]. This was the question of preponderance of Sunni and Shiahs with special reference to question of constitutional (assembly) shortly to be convened. As we [British] were aware there was already technical and numerical preponderance of Shiahs and excision of their representatives from National Assembly would place Shiahs in a very strong position and filled him [Faysal] with misgiving.

The policies implicit in Faysal's statement of September 1921 were to be made explicit by the Iraq government and Britain up to the time of the final negotiations between Turkey, Iraq and Britain culminating in the 5 June 1926 Treaty. These policies were followed essentially to 1958. The question of the relationship between Sunni and Shi'i Arabs and between

Sunnis and Kurds was to be the centerpiece of the governance of Iraq up to the revolution in 1958. It should be mentioned in this regard that Sir Percy Cox was instrumental in pushing the Iraq boundary as far north as it is today. Many Foreign Office officials were willing to grant Turkey more territory than the High Commissioner. For example, the Foreign Office in 1926 was willing to let Amadiya revert to Turkey. In the final stages of the negotiations for the 1926 treaty, both the Foreign Office and the Air Ministry were willing to allow the border between Turkey and Iraq to descend to the hills immediately north of Ruwanduz in order to persuade Turkey to speedily conclude the treaty. The Air Ministry's officers were the commanders of Iraq's armed forces and heads of intelligence.

Sir Henry Dobbs, who replaced Cox as High Commissioner in 1923, was as emphatic as his predecessor that the Sunni Kurds were necessary to preserve Sunni domination of the Iraqi government. On 15 March 1925, Sir Ronald Lindsay, British ambassador to Turkey and the principal negotiator in the British-Turkish talks, in order to arrive at a final resolution of the Mosul question and eager to make the necessary territorial concessions to the Turks that he thought would conclude the treaty, asked Dobbs if he would agree with the grant of a "considerable" tract of land to Turkey in order to conclude the negotiations. On 16 March, one day after his conversation with Lindsay, Dobbs explained his objections to accede further territory to Turkey. He gave strategical, tactical and political reasons as to why Turkey should not be granted more territory in northern Iraq.

> The Kurds in the tracts which Turkey desires have been the short anchor of British influence in Iraq. It was only through the solid pro-British Kurdish 'bloc' in the constituent assembly that the Anglo-Iraq Treaty was accepted in June 1924. And since then they have consistently supported British policy by their votes and influence...a cession of loyal Kurdish tracts to Turkey would engender mistrust of us throughout Iraq, not only among the Kurds but among the Arabs. It would make our position well nigh impossible and would weaken Iraq far more than the pressure of an unappeased Turkey on her borders.

Dobbs then went on to stress the negative effects of the cession of "considerable" tracts of land to Turkey on the ruling Sunni class in Iraq.

The cession of considerable Kurdish tracts to Turkey would enrage and disgust the ruling Arab class in Iraq, who are all Sunnis. For it would upset the balance in the Iraq parliament against the Sunnis and put the retrograde and obscurantist Shiahs into power. Rather than this should happen, the well disposed Arab Sunni moderates such as Abdul Mubsin, the present P.M. [prime minister] would prefer to return to Turkey altogether.

Dobb's statement makes clear that in his view, Kurdish support was absolutely necessary to insure the domination of parliament by the elite Sunni classes under the aegis of the British. It was necessary to maintain this balance even at the *risk of alienating Turkey* (author's italics). In addition it is clear that the High Commissioner had a low opinion of the Shi'is. Dobbs was extremely influential in determining British policy in Iraq during this tenure as High Commissioner from 1923 to 1929. During his six year term, nearly all of the policies he presented to the Colonial and Foreign Office were implemented.

What is important for our topic here is that it is clear from the evidence that after March 1922, and the circumstances surrounding the signing of the Treaty of Lausanne (24 July 1923) provide strong support of this, British policy did not favor the creation of *any kind of Kurdish state for a host of geopolitic and geostrategic reasons* (author's italics).

The needs of the British empire to dominate the Middle East via Iraq, and to gain the cooperation of the new states of Turkey and Iran did not favor the establishment of a Kurdish state after WW I. Many of these same geopolitic and geostrategic circumstances were still factors in the forces that were opposed to the creation of a Kurdish state after the Persian Gulf war. Some scholars contend that the United States and Europe, especially the former, did not want to create a Kurdish state in northern Iraq after the Persian Gulf war, but only a strong enough entity to be able to deter Saddam Husayn's regime in Baghdad. What is important in the following essay is that the governments of Turkey, Iran and Syria and the weakened government of Iraq *all believed that it was the policy of the United States to try to establish a Kurdish state in northern Iraq* (author's italics). All four states, in spite of great differences among them, cooperated in making sure that such a state or even a strong autonomous entity would not emerge in northern Iraq. The two states most involved in crushing this perceived threat were Turkey and Iran. They did so because the creation of a Kurdish state or even a strong Kurdish entity in northern Iraq was thought to be dangerous to the geopolitical and geostrategical interests of both countries. My essay seeks to explain what those interests were and are.

CHAPTER ONE

The Theoretical Setting and the Historical Kurdish Question in Turkey

The Theoretical Setting

This study has as its topic the Kurdish question and Turkey-Iran relations from WW I to 1998 and includes brief commentary on the role of the Kurdish question during the imperial phase of the two states' relations. In this study the *Kurdish question* refers to the trans-state aspects of the Kurdish nationalist movement and the *Kurdish problem* refers to the domestic challenge that the Kurdish nationalist movement presents to Turkey and Iran.

There is no international relations theory that addresses adequately the functioning of either Turkey or Iran in the world political system or even within the Middle East. One of the most suitable theories is that of "omni-balancing."[1] Omni-balancing incorporates the essential elements of balance of power theories of the neorealist school but differs in emphasizing that third world states, and especially leaders of such states, would rather deal cooperatively with secondary adversaries so that they can focus their resources on adversaries they deem more threatening. In order to do so they seek to split the alignment against them and to appease the international allies of their domestic opponents.[2] The essential aspect of omni-balancing is that alignment decisions of third world leaders cannot be understood without reference to the role of internal threats to the

---

[1]Steven R. David, "Explaining Third World Alignment," *World Politics*, vol. 43, no. 2 (1991):233-56.

[2]Good examples of this are the attempts of Turkey and Iran to declare to international human rights organizations that they are in compliance with international human rights standards regarding their policies toward the Kurds.

leadership. In the following analysis, I employ the omni-balancing model with the exception that in the case of Turkey and Iran the states themselves rather than simply the leaders should be the focus of alignment structures. The most salient aspect of omni-balancing is that, unlike realist and neorealist models, it concentrates on internal threats to the regime.[3]

The theory of omni-balancing postulates that third world countries reproduce rather than provide havens from the anarchy of international politics: third world politics are a microcosm of international politics. Balancing is as critical for groups within states as it is between states. Unlike balance of power theories, omni-balancing suggests that third world states construct their alignments on their perceptions of how to best protect themselves from threats they face, whether the source is domestic or international. The "safe haven" established for the Kurds by Allied forces led by thc U.S. in the wake of the 1991 Persian Gulf war is a good example of the reproduction of "anarchy" rather than tranquility in world politics.

Omni-balancing again differs from balance of power theory which holds "states that are driven by internal threats are likely to be weak, in which case they will not affect the global balance of power anyway."[4] I argue here that Turkey and Iran are not weak states and that their inability to contain the Kurdish nationalist movement, especially the creation of an independent Kurdish state, would affect the global balance of power.

In a recent study Anoushiravan Ehteshami and Raymond Hinnebusch argue that Syria and Iran are middle ranking powers in a penetrated regional system.[5] They define regional middle powers as states that rank as middle powers in the global system but which are key actors in their regional systems. The two authors posit that middle powers such as Iran and Syria are "distinguishable from lesser regional powers by their

---

[3]For a review of these models see Robert O. Keohane, ed., *Neorealism and Its Critics* (New York: Columbia University Press, 1986). The thesis of this book is that the Kurdish nationalist movements have constituted major threats to Iran and to Turkey and, in the case of Turkey, the major threat, to the state since its founding in 1923.

[4]David, 253.

[5]Anoushiravan Ehteshami and Raymond A. Hinnesbusch, *Syria and Iran: Middle Powers in a Penetrated Regional System* (London: Routledge, 1997).

assertion of regional leadership in the name of more general interests, by their centrality to the regional power balance, their regional spheres of influence and by their ability, from a credible deterrent capability, to resist a coalition of other regional states against them. Finally, such powers generally have leaders enjoying more than local stature and some extra-regional influence."[6] In the analysis below, I argue that Turkey also fulfills all of these criteria.

Other characteristics of regional middle powers are that they are still economically and technologically dependent on the core and that in order to reduce their dependency they must diversify their economies. Most important, in the case of Turkey and Iran (and Syria), regional powers are potential barriers to the globalization of superpower hegemony. Even though Iran currently fulfills this role more closely than Turkey because of the latter's pro-West policies, it also could be a potential barrier to superpower hegemony.

Middle level powers are generally able to escape diplomatic isolation and military intervention at the hands of great powers since the latter may need their support against rivals, and even a hostile great power will normally be deterred (by the likely costs) from attacking a middle power.[7] In keeping with middle powers' aspirations, Turkey and Iran seek to maximize their autonomy by balancing the regional impact of great powers: the greater the penetration of the big powers, the stronger the efforts of regional powers, such as Turkey and Iran, to limit this penetration. In the past twenty years this effort has been much stronger on the part of Iran than Turkey.

I argue, as Ehteshami and Hinnebusch do for Iran and Syria, that Turkey operates in a region that historically has been and still is a penetrated region. The region has been penetrated historically for great powers' goals ranging from economic hegemony, including monopolizing oil resources to the preservation of Israel after 1948. Indeed, one can argue that the end of bipolarity in the late 1980s has increased the penetration of the indigenous states of the Middle East, Balkans, Caucasus and Central Asia regions, in which Turkey and Iran see themselves as playing major roles.

Both Turkey and Iran follow a bureaucratic politics model in which

---

[6]*Ibid.* 6-7.

[7]*Ibid.*

foreign policy is made by competing elites with different interests. The state needs the support of internal classes, and public opinion does play a role. In such a model, foreign policy is a weapon in domestic political struggles. The role that the Kurdish question and Kurdish problem have played in Turkey's politics since the end of the Persian Gulf war is a good example of this model. The bureaucratic model also stresses that the top executive has the capability of arbitrating between factions which allows "the autonomy to omni-balance in pursuit of a rational foreign policy."[8] Prior to the Islamic revolution, Iran's foreign policy is better characterized by the autonomous unitary elite theory, such as currently prevails in Syria.

The thesis of this essay is that omni-balancing is the model that best characterizes Turkey's and Iran's foreign and domestic policies and that the Kurdish question and Kurdish problem play paramount roles in this model. I argue below that they have played the dominant role in Turkey's foreign and domestic policy since 1991, and that they have played major roles, but not paramount ones, in Iran's foreign policy since the Persian Gulf war.[9]

The Historical Kurdish Question in Turkey

The role of the Kurds in Middle East and Islamic history has always been an important and in many ways a determinative one. This is especially true in the case of Iran and Turkey. The very origins of the Ottoman and Safavid empires and their subsequent configurations was in substantial ways affected by the presence of the Kurds in the frontier regions of both empires. The Kurds and the territories they occupied were among the crucial differences between the two empires until their collapse in the first quarter of the twentieth century. (See maps 1 and 2). One of the determining factors for Kurdish history in this important rivalry was that the bulk of them opted in favor of the Ottoman empire.[10] Recent

---

[8]*Ibid.* 21.

[9]It is important to note that in scholarly literature dealing with the Middle East there are two Persian Gulf wars: The first between Iran and Iraq (1980-1988) and the second of the U.S. led Allied forces in 1991.

[10]Mehrad R. Izady, *A Concise Handbook: The Kurds* (Washington: Crane Russel, 1992), 72, provides a bibliography for this period, see especially his references to the *Encyclopedia of Islam.*

scholarship in particular emphasizes the critical role of the Kurds in Ottoman history, especially in its relations with the Safavids and the two empires' competition to achieve dominance over Islamic discourse in the dialectics of Sunni-Shi'i rivalry.[11]

The Ottoman and Safavid competition for territories was settled as a result of the Treaty of Kasr-i Shirin, sometimes referred to as the Treaty of Zuhab, and significantly called the "Treaty of Peace and Frontiers," signed on 17 May 1639. Rouhallah K. Ramazani is of the opinion that the treaty of 1639 reflected a significant change in Iran's policy. He suggests that "The two Muslim states invoked the Islamic precept `Fear God and reconcile yourselves' while they were actually for the first time basing their relations on territorial considerations and establishing boundaries between themselves."[12]

The significant point to be made is that, with the exception of small modifications in the boundaries between Turkey and Iran as a result of the 1932 treaty, the boundaries between the Ottoman, Safavid and Qajar empires as well as the boundaries of the modern republics of Turkey and Iran have remained almost the same since 1639. The changes that did occur resulted from boundary disputes in the Caucasus. Territories occupied by Kurds and demarcated by the treaties of 1639 and 1932, notably one between empires and the other between independent countries,

---

[11]For the social and economic rivalry behind the discoursive religious competition see Robert Olson, *The Siege of Mosul and Ottoman-Persian Relations, 1718-1747* (Bloomington: Indiana University Press, 1975); Robert Dankoff, *The Intimate Life of an Ottoman Statesman: Melek Ahmed Paşa as Portrayed in Evliya Çelebi's Book of Travels* (Albany: State University of New York, 1991); Martin van Bruinessen and Hendrik Boeschaten, *Evliya Çelebi in Diyarbekir* (Leiden: E. J. Brill, 1988). Izady is of the opinion that developments in the sixteenth and seventeenth centuries played a decisive role in Kurdish history in that they effected a "fundamental cultural realignment, from the dominance of the sedentary, mainly Pahlâwani-speaking Kurds, to the prevalence of the nomadic, primarily Kurmanji-speaking Kurds in northern and western Kurdistan" (*Handbook*, 103). This is a process that had begun earlier as a consequence of a shift in the international trade routes resulting from the circumnavigation of the Cape of Good Hope.

[12]The text of the treaty is in J.C. Hurewitz, *Diplomacy in the Near and Middle East* (Princeton: C. van Nostrand, 1956), vol. I, 21-3; Rouhollah K. Ramazani, *The Foreign Policy of Iran: A Developing Nation in World Affairs, 1500-1941* (Charlottesville: University Press of Virginia, 1966).

have also lasted to the present. (See map 3). The major changes in the boundaries between Turkey and Iran as demarcated in 1639 came about in the Caucasus as a result of Russian annexation and are embodied in the Treaty of Gülistan of 1813 and the Treaty of Turkomanchay of 1828. (See map 4). The foreign policy approaches of the Ottoman, Safavid and Qajar empires were very much characterized by the omni-balancing alignment paradigm mentioned earlier.

Much has been written recently regarding Kurdish nationalist movements in Turkey, Iran and Iraq.[13] There is no need here to review the scholarly literature on the origins of Kurdish, Turkish and Iranian nationalism. There is consensus among scholars that Turkish nationalism as an ideological movement began in the first decade of the twentieth century during the Young Turk period.[14] Persian nationalism as distinct from Iraninan nationalism was developed before the twentieth century, although it became more defined with the establishment of the Pahlavi dynasty in 1925. The periodization of Kurdish nationalism is more problematic than either Turkish or Iranian nationalism. The current debate regarding the emergence of Kurdish nationalism pivots on whether the Sheikh Said rebellion of 1925 was more of a nationalist or a religious movement. The attempt to periodize the development of Kurdish nationalism is important as it contributes to the greater understanding not only of Kurdish history but also of the history of Turkey and Iran in the interwar period and the contours of post WW I Middle Eastern historiography.[15]

---

[13]Here I shall give just a few of the main titles. The best overview of the history of the Kurds is David McDowall, *A Modern History of the Kurds* (London: I. B. Tauris, 1996); Martin van Bruinessen, *Agha, Shaikh and State: The Social and Political Structures of Kurdistan* (London: Zed Books, 1992); Wadie Jwaideh, The Kurdish Nationalist Movement: Its Origins and Development (University of Syracuse, PhD diss. 1960); Robert Olson, *The Emergence of Kurdish Nationalism and the Sheikh Said Rebellion, 1880-1925* (Austin: University of Texas Press, 1989) and Amir Hassanpour, *Nationalism and Language in Kurdistan* (San Francisco: Mellen Research University Press, 1992).

[14]M. Şükrü Hanioğlu, *The Young Turks in Opposition* (New York: Oxford University Press, 1995), 212 states, "The CUP [Committee of Union and Progress]'s shift to nationalism and securement of the military's endorsement was realized in 1905."

[15]For a review of different opinions regarding the nationalist content of the

Nearly all of the literature dealing with the origins of Kurdish nationalism emphasizes the pivotal role played by the Sheikh Said rebellion in raising the political consciousness of the Kurds in Turkey. The Sheikh Said rebellion also seems to have been the paramount development in the Turkish government's realization that Kurdish nationalism, even in its embryonic state, could prove to be a serious threat to the Turkish ethnic-based nationalism that the Kemalists were instituting in the 1920s.[16] Indeed, from 1925 onward the Turkish government waged continued warfare against the Kurds. There were major wars again in 1930 and 1937-38. The suppression of the Kurds in the 1937-38 war in Dersim, present day Tunceli, was so great that scholars have referred to it as genocide and/or ethnocide.[17] One of the major factors contributing to the success of the suppression of Kurdish rebellions from 1930 to the present was the development of the Turkish air force, which by 1930 already comprised some 300 aircraft.[18]

Sheikh Said rebellion see Robert Olson, "The Kurdish Rebellions of Sheikh Said (1925), Mt. Ararat (1930) and Dersim (1937-38): Their Impact on the Development of the Turkish Air Force and on Kurdish and Turkish Nationalism," *Die Welt des Islams* (forthcoming).

[16]One of the latest officially sanctioned government reports, *The Southeast Report (Güney Doğu Raporu*, prepared by a research team under the direction of Doğu Ergil, a professor of political science at Ankara University, analyzes the current, (i.e., 1990s), discontent among the Kurds in southeastern Turkey, proffering solutions to Turkey's Kurdish problem. The report stresses the significance of the Sheikh Said rebellion in "developing the fear of Kurdish nationalism among the nationalists." *Hürriyet*, 20 August 1995.

[17]For a review of Turkish attempts to assimilate the Kurds see McDowall, 184-213; İsmail Beşikçi, *Tunceli kanunu (1935) ve Dersim Jinosidi* (İstanbul: Belge Yayınları, 1990), especially pages 95-7 in which Beşikçi characterizes Turkish actions in Dersim as genocide. Martin van Bruninessen, "Genocide in Kurdistan? The Suppression of the Dersim Rebellion in Turkey (1937-38) and the Chemical War Against the Iraqi Kurds (1988)," in *Genocide: Conceptual and Historical Dimensions*, ed. George J. Andreapoulos (Philadelphia: University of Pennsylvania, 1994), considers that Turkey's actions against the Kurds in Dersim did not constitute genocide but they do qualify as ethnocide, "the destruction of Kurdish ethnic identity" (148).

[18]Olson, "Kurdish Rebellions ..." (forthcoming in *Die Welt des Islams*).

The significance of the Kurdish rebellions of 1925, 1930 and 1937-38 and the role they played in the consolidation of an ethnic-based Turkish nationalism and the concomitant weakening of Kurdish nationalism is perhaps best illustrated by statements made by the highest ranking Turkish officials in the aftermath of each rebellion.

In April 1925 after the crushing of Sheikh Said's rebellion and just after the capture of the Sheikh himself, İsmet İnönü, the Turkish prime minister, made the following statement:

> We are frankly Nationalist...and Nationalism is our factor of cohesion. Before the Turkish majority other elements have no kind of influence. At any price, we must turkify the inhabitants of our land, and we will annihilate those who oppose Turks and "le turquisme." What we seek in those who would serve the country is that, above all, they be Turks and "turquistes." They say we lack solicitude for religious currents; we will crush all who rise before us to use religion as an instrument.[19]

Forty years later, İnönü had still not changed his mind. In an interview with the well known Turkish journalist Abdi İpekçi, the long-time foreign minister of Turkey said, "The destiny of the regime in domestic politics and in the military arena was absolutely dependent on a definite and positive result in the rebellion in the East."[20]

Five years after İnönü's 1925 statement and during Turkey's suppression of the Kurdish rebellion around Mt. Ararat, Mahmud Esad Bozkurt, the Turkish interior minister, made his well known declaration:

> Only the Turkish nation has the privilege of demanding national rights in this country. There is no possibility that other ethnic groups' demands for such a right will be

---

[19]Bilâl N. Şimşir, ed., *İngiliz Belgeleriyle Türkiye'de "Kürt Sorunu (1924-1938: Şeyh Said, Ağrı ve Dersim Ayaklamaları"* (Ankara: Türk Tarih Kurumu, 1991), 2nd ed., 58. This quotation was included in a dispatch from British Ambassador to Turkey Sir Ronald Lindsay to Foreign Secretary Austin Chamberlain dated 28 April 1925, no. 331 found in Foreign Office *Confidential Print Series*, series no. 424, no. 262, 156-7. İnönü made the address to the Türk Ocakları in Ankara on 21 April 1925.

[20]Abdi İpekçi, *İnönü Atatürk'ü Anlatıyor* (İstanbul: Am Yayın Evi, 1981), 27.

recognized. There is no need to hide the truth. The Turks are the sole owners and the sole notables of this country. Those who are not of Turkish origin have only one right: to serve and to be the slaves without question, of the noble Turkish nation.[21]

After the crushing of the Dersim rebellion in 1938, Atatürk, just a few months before his death, gave a speech in which he said that he was happy to announce that " we have not allowed and will not allow any possibility that might create an obstacle able to prevent our nation from achieving the high level of civilization and happiness that it merits."[22]

The above statements made after the Turkish government's defeat of the three major Kurdish rebellions prior to WW II represent the great significance that the highest ranking Turkish leaders attached to the suppression of the rebellions in order to emphasize the Turkish ethnic base of Turkish nationalism and of Kemalism. The suppression of the three interwar rebellions contributed strongly to the unchallenged development of Turkish nationalist discourse with increasingly strident emphasis on Turkish ethnicity. The suppression of the Kurds, their forced emigration and the ethnic cleansing they endured made it impossible for them to mount a challenge against the increasingly monodimensional Turkish nationalism.

---

[21]This Passage quoted from İhsan Nouri Pasha, *Ağrı Dağı Isyanı*, 103. Bozkurt's statement appeard originally in the *Milliyet* newspaper on 19 September 1930.

[22]Hamit Bozarslan, "Le Kemalisme et le problem kurde," in *Les kurdes de là l'exode*, ed. H. Hakim (Paris: Éditions L'Hartmattan, 1992, 76 relying on Celal Kutay, *Celal Bayar*, vol. 3 (İstanbul: Keran Yayın Evi, 1938), 1,354.

CHAPTER TWO

The Historical Kurdish Question in Iran

The experiences of the Kurds and of Kurdish tribes in Iran differed from that of the Ottoman empire. The political-military alliance the Ottomans forged with the Kurds after 1514 was to the detriment of the Safavid empire. The Safavids (1501-1724) and their successors, the Qajars (1795-1925), did not want to repeat such an experience. Subsequently, their policy was to destroy or weaken the Kurdish principalities. As a result, the Kurdish tribes were subjected to stricter political and looser financial control than other tribes in Iran. Abbas Vali maintains that, "the main aim of this policy was to ensure the political and military support of the Kurdish tribes in the cross-border relations with the Ottoman state, while preventing the formation of large and powerful tribal confederations in Iranian Kurdistan."[23] Vali contends that the destruction of the Kurdish principalities resulted in a tribalization of Kurdish urban centers. This practice continued until the end of the nineteenth century when the tribal chiefs were replaced with members of the Qajar family. This is an interesting development as far as the topic of this article is concerned in that this change of policy may have been due in part to the consequences of Sheikh Ubaydallah's movement in 1880-81. Although Sheikh Ubaydallah's movement is not considered a nationalist movement, it is an example of a strong Kurdish movement to achieve greater autonomy.[24]

---

[23] Abbas Vali, "The Making of Kurdish Identity in Iran," *Critique*, no. 7 (1995), 10. This article originally appeared in French as "Genèse et structure du nationalisme kurde en Iran," in *Peuples Méditerranéens*, nos. 68-69 (1994):143-64.

[24] Again, like the Sheikh Said rebellion in Turkey, the scholarly debate is whether Sheikh Ubaydallah's rebellion was nationalistic. Most scholars nowadays think that it was not. In addition to Vali, see McDowall, 53-9; Olson, *The Emergence of Kurdish Nationalism*, 1-7.

For the purposes of this article, the rebellion is significant in that it occurred largely in Kurdish territories of Turkey and Iran. It took 12,000 Iranian troops to crush the rebellion, and it caused considerable diplomatic tension between the Ottoman and Qajar governments. The Iranians thought that the Ottomans had instigated the rebellion of Ubaydallah for the purpose of using his Kurdish League against the development of Armenian nationalism in their eastern territories. The significance of Ubaydallah's rebellion and his Kurdish movement is that it demonstrated that the demands of Kurds, whether nationalist or not, posed a formidable challenge to the major states in which they resided.

Agha Simko's rebellion is another important expression of the Kurdish question in Iran. The question of whether he and the rebellion he led were or were not nationalist is again controversial. Nader Entessar thinks Simko's revolt was "the first major attempt by the Kurds to establish an independent Kurdistan." Martin van Bruinessen views it as a nationalist rebellion, although not sharply different from "the more traditional tribal rebellion." David McDowall opines that Simko's nationalism was more defined by socio-economic status than by ethnicity. Abbas Vali on the other hand emphasizes that the rebellion was "essentially tribal and autonomist."[25] The important consequence of Simko Agha's rebellion for our topic is that Reza Shah's government treated it as if it were a *nationalist* rebellion because it threatened the state.

Reza Shah's repression of the Kurdish tribes and of tribal leadership in the wake of Simko's rebellion was severe and drastic enough that when the Kurds again rebelled in 1944-46 it was an urban-based, rather than a tribally based, Kurdish nationalism that played the important role in the creation of the Kurdish Republic of Mahabad, the first and only Kurdish state to be established yet. Abbas Vali argues that the suppression of Kurdish identity during the Reza Shah period "was intrinsic to the self-definition of the emergent nationalist state in Iran." It was "this forced identity and insistence on the expression of their difference that laid the foundation for the emergence of Kurdish nationalism in Iranian Kurdistan." Vali attributes the formation of the *Komola-i Jeyanawa-i Kurdistan* (Society for the Revival of Kurdistan) in 1942 as marking the

---

[25]For a review of this question see McDowall, 214-23; Nader Entessar, *Kurdish Ethnonationalism* (Boulder: Lynne Rienner, 1992), 12-3; Martin van Bruinessen, "Kurdish Tribes and the State in Iran: The Case of Simko's Revolt," in *The Conflict of Tribe and State in Iran and Afghanistan* (London: Croom-Helm, 1983), 364-99.

advent of modern nationalist "thought and practice in Iranian Kurdistan."[26] Komala assumed the title Democratic Party of Kurdistan in 1944 and played the leading role in the establishment of the Kurdish Republic of Mahabad, which lasted from December 1945 to December 1946.

The suppression of the Kurdish rebellions in the interwar period in both Turkey and Iran demonstrated the similar consequences for the development of Kurdish nationalism in both states: the suppression of Kurdish identity was intrinsic to the self-definition of both Turkish and Iranian nationalism. The still nascent development of both Turkish and Iranian nationalism impelled governing officials in both countries to assert hegemonical control over national discourse centered on Turkish and Iranian ethnic identity.

Post-WW I Turkish and Iranian Cooperation Against the Kurds

The parallel concerns of both states led increasingly to their efforts and eventually treaties to control their Kurdish borderlands. As early as 1920 Iran was concerned about "the developments in the Kurdish territory of the neighboring Ottoman state, and especially watchful of the Kurdish representation and consideration of the Kurdish question in the League of Nations."[27]   The Iranian representative to the League advised the government of Tehran to adopt a policy of cultural assimilation rather than political coercion and suppression of Kurdish ethnic identity.   In 1927 the Iranian government was so shaken by the scale and strength of Sheikh Said's rebellion and the destabilizing effects of Simko's activities that it proposed joint Iranian-Turkish cooperation against Kurdish movements. During the same year, the Turkish army still fighting the rebel Kurds, who had fought in the Sheikh Said rebellion, pursued the rebels into Iranian territory to capture them, but instead the Turkish soldiers were captured by the Kurds. Ankara thought the captured Turks had been sent to Tehran on orders of the Iranian government and protested by withdrawing its ambassador. The first withdrawal of an ambassador occurred, notably, as a result of the Kurdish question.[28]

---

[26]Vali, 17-8.

[27]*Ibid.* 15.

[28]Tschanguiz H. Pahlavan, "Turkish-Iranian Relations: An Iranian View," in Henri J. Barkey, ed. *Reluctant Neighbor: Turkey's Role in the Middle East*

Throughout the 1920s Kurds, whether to seek refuge or to play one state against another, passed freely from one state to another. Many of the Kurds who fled Turkish suppression after the 1925 and 1930 rebellions fled to Iran as well as Iraq. Simko Agha found refuge in Turkey and Iraq before he was assassinated by the Iranian army on 21 June 1930. The policy of assassinating Kurdish leaders or potential leaders was a policy that Iranian governments pursued up to 1992. In 1928 Simko left for Turkey apparently "lured by the promise of a regiment of tribal cavalry and the award of an estate on the Iranian frontier."[29] He was assassinated probably because Tehran viewed Ankara's use of him as a threat to its border area and decided to kill him.

During the Kurdish rebellion around Mt. Ararat in the summer of 1930, the Turks threatened constantly to bomb Iran's territory if it did not stop supporting the Kurdish rebels which Ankara alleged it was doing. The Turks even built an airstrip to accommodate 100 aircraft just a few kilometers from the Iranian border.[30] The rebellion received at least tacit and probably some actual support from Iran. Iran allowed Kurdish forces to cross freely into its territories after they were defeated in the fall of 1930 after heavy air bombardment. Nader Entessar is of the opinion that Reza Shah "apparently was intent on using his 'Kurdish card' to force Turkey to settle some of its territorial disputes with Iran."[31] The Kurdish rebels, led by İhsan Nouri Pasha, who also played a key role in Sheikh Said's rebellion, received equipment and supplies from Iranian Kurdistan and Azerbaijan.

The Ararat rebellion is a milestone for Turkey-Iran relations and the Kurdish question. It led to the signing of the Turko-Iran Frontier Treaty on 23 January 1932 that, with the addition of a small adjustment in 1937, still obtains. The 1932 treaty was made to satisfy Turkey's need to control the eastern slopes of Mt. Ararat where the Kurds had so thoroughly ensconced themselves during the rebellion. In return for ceding the eastern slopes, Iran received small strips of land near Kotur

---

(Washington, D.C.: United States Insitute of Peace Press, 1996), 72.

[29]McDowall, 221.

[30]Olson, "Kurdish Rebellions..," see note 18. I used as my source the newspaper *Cumhuriyet*, April-September 1930.

[31]Entessar, 85.

and Bazirgan. In 1937 Iran was given a small favorable adjustment near Maz Bicho, west of Urmia.[32]

The two countries also signed a Treaty of Conciliation, Judicial Settlement and Arbitration on 23 January 1932. These two treaties were followed by the Treaty of Friendship signed on 5 November 1932. The three treaties "constituted the new bases of Iran's relations with Turkey."[33] The Kurdish question, then, was the paramount factor determining the final boundary between the two countries. The relationship established between Ankara and Tehran by the treaties of 1932 to control the activities of the Kurds was enforced to the Iran-Iraq war (1980-1988) and into the 1990s. After the Persian Gulf war in 1991, however, there were new negotiations to control the activities of the PKK or *Partia Karkaren Kurdistan*, the militant Kurdish nationalist organization in Turkey that had implanted itself more strongly in northern Iraq and northern Iran after the Persian Gulf war. These developments will be discussed below.

The treaties of 1932 were reconfirmed by the Treaty of Non-Aggression known as the Sadaabad Pact named after the Shah's summer palace in north Tehran where the pact was signed on 8 July 1937. Afghanistan and Iraq were also signees. With the exception of Afghanistan, the major concern of the participants was the Kurdish challenge. Of the core ten articles of the treaty, four dealt directly with the need to control the Kurds, a remarkable fact considering the treaty was announced as a way to protect the signees from an "external" attack.[34]

The Sadaabad Pact occurred while Turkey was in the midst of crushing the Dersim rebellion, the third major Kurdish rebellion in Turkey during the interwar period. Unlike the Sheikh Said and Mt. Ararat rebellions, the Dersim rebellion did not occur near the Iranian border and hence the usual problems of cross border incursions and Iranian support for the rebels did not occur. Abbas Vali thinks that one of the objectives of the Sadaabad Pact was to "regionalize the Kurdish question in the context of an anti-communist alliance" that in itself signified "the persistence of an anxiety about the possible threat Kurdish ethnicity could

---

[32]McDowall, 206; Entessar, 85; Maria T. O'Shea, "The Question of Kurdistan and Iran's International Borders," *The Borders of Iran*, ed. Keith McLachan (New York: St. Martin's Press, 1994), 54.

[33]Ramazani, 272.

[34]For an abridged text of the treaty see Hurewitz vol. II, 214-7.

pose to Turkey or Iran [and Iraq] should the regional conditions prove favorable."[35]

The Creation and Impact of the Kurdish Republic of Mahabad

The treaties of 1932 and 1937 were not affected by the creation of the Kurdish Republic of Mahabad which lasted for exactly one year-December 1945 to December 1946. Recent scholarship stresses that the the establishment of the Mahabad republic was motivated primarily by Kurdish nationalism.[36] The establishment and destruction of the Mahabad Republic was largely a Kurdish nationalist development that affected the Kurds in Iran and Iraq. It did not directly affect Iran-Turkish relations, although Ankara was undoubtedly delighted to learn of the republic's destruction by Mohammad Reza, the new Shah of Iran. The Turks hoped that the new Shah would be as cooperative against the Kurds as the old Shah had been. The Mahabad Republic, however, did affect the Kurds of Turkey because, as Nader Entessar has pointed out, "it has remained the point of reference for Kurdish movements throughout the Middle East."[37] The Mahabad Republic was inspirational to the fledgling Kurdish nationalist movements in Turkey. Another worrying aspect of the Mahabad Republic was that for the first time since the 1920 Treaty of Sèvres, the Kurdish question had become fully internationalized: it would not become so again until 1991. The fact that the Mahabad Republic along with the Democratic Republic of Azerbaijan played a significant role in the commencement of the cold war attests further to its significance internationally rather than just for Kurdish, Iranian, Turkish or Iraqi history. Great Britain in particular did not want to see the creation of an independent Kurdish state in the Middle East. In fact, it seems unlikely that Britain desired even a strong autonomous Kurdish zone in Iran, Iraq or Turkey. British support for a bland and bureaucratic Kurdish nationalism in northern Iraq was necessary for London to pursue in the Arab countries of the Middle East its Sharifian policy that supposed moderate Arab nationalism would have been jeopardized by a strong Kurdish nationalist movement in either Iran or Turkey.

---

[35]Vali, 15, n. 21.

[36]McDowall, 246; Vali, 18-22; Entessar, 14-23.

[37]Entessar, 22.

By 1945 Britain, the U.S. and Europe had already decided that Turkey would be a potential ally against the Soviet Union and the spread of communism in the Middle East. These realizations were implemented in the Truman Doctrine in 1946-47 and influenced Turkey's admission to NATO in 1952. Kurdish communists' participation in communist and other leftist parties in the Middle East was also considered a danger. The Mahabad Republic represented the same threat that the Sheikh Said rebellion had twenty years earlier in Turkey: both were led by religious leaders. The leaders of Turkey, Iran and Iraq as well as Great Britain, the latter the hegemonical imperial power of the time, did not want any mixture of Islam and nationalism. The newly created states of Iran and Turkey also did not want any such mixture. As mentioned above, İsmet İnönü made it emphatically clear in 1925 that "We [the Turks] shall crush all who rise before us to use religion as an instrument."

I have written elsewhere that the suppression of the Sheikh Said rebellion reduced the utility of Islam as a vehicle of challenge and/or opposition not only in Turkey but also to other governments in the Middle East. Groups who wished to use Islam as an instrument of cooperation with other Muslim states or to include it in other international objectives also found its effectiveness diminished.[38] The suppression of any nationalist group, ethnic or otherwise, who attempted to use Islam as a vehicle to challenge the regimes in power was perhaps the main objective of all of the governments of the central Middle East (I exclude Afghanistan and Pakistan here) which emphasized secularism as the basis of their legitimacy right up to 1998. The sole exception was Iran, where an Islamic based government came into power after 1979.[39] In Turkey the anti-Kurdish nationalist and anti-Islamist nationalist policies, the latter of which included some Kurdish nationalists, continues up to the present. In 1997 the first party, the Welfare party (WP) led by Necmettin Erbakan, which assumed power in June 1996 in coalition with the True Path Party (TPP) led by former Prime Minister Tansu Çiller, was toppled from power by the Turkish Armed Forces (TAF) which proclaimed the WP

---

[38]Olson, *The Emergence of Kurdish Nationalism*, 151-3.

[39]I use the term *Islamic* in referring to the 1979 revolution in Iran because of the role that orthodox values and symbols played in the revolutionary discourse. I use the term *Islamist* to refer to the religious-political movements in the Middle East and in Iran and Turkey that do not necessarily rely on the traditional and orthodox symbols and discourse.

"reactionary" (irticai). Indeed, in 1997, for the first time in a decade and a half, the TAF, who determine Turkey's security policies and much else in the country, stressed that the number one enemy of the state was not the PKK but rather the WP and the Islamist "reactionism" it represented. The greatest challenge to the Kemalist Turkish state announced the TAF and the subsequent right-wing government of the Motherland Party (MP) that came to power on 20 June, "was not the PKK but the cooperation between the Islamists and the PKK and/or other Kurdish nationalist groups."[40]

From 1932 to the Islamic revolution in Iran in 1979, there was no official support by Ankara or Tehran for Kurdish nationalist movements within either country. After the Islamic revolution both governments repeatedly stated that they did not support Kurdish nationalist organizations in their respective countries. Ankara's and Tehran's respective "Kurdish cards" were to be dealt in playing with and against the two principal Kurdish organizations in Iraq: the Kurdistan Democratic Party (KDP), led by Ma'sud Barzani, and the Patriotic Union of Kurdistan (PUK), led by Jalal Talabani. Tehran also supported the Islamic Movement of Kurdistan (IMK), led by Shaykh 'Uthman of Ranya, a region in northern Iraq close to the Iranian border.

I argue that the geopolitic and geostrategic concerns of Turkey and Iran from 1920 to 1978 were so paramount that neither wanted each other or any other country or external organization to jeopardize their larger geopolitical interests by supporting Kurdish nationalist organizations or movements or by inciting the Kurds to rebellion, terrorism or war. Even in the 1990s, when it seemed clear that Tehran was providing the PKK with support within Iraq, Iran and in Europe, and that Ankara was providing support within Turkey and Iraq to the *mojahedin-i halq*, the stongest oppositional group to the Iranian regime, both countries strove to maintain "plausible deniability."

---

[40]*Hürriyet*, 11 June 1997.

CHAPTER THREE

From the Islamic Revolution to the Persian Gulf War: 1979-1991

Turkey had two primary concerns with the Islamic revolution in Iran. One was the worry that the latter's Islamist currents would infect Turkey; the other concern was that the failure of the revolution and the subsequent fragmentation of Iran would lead to the establishment of a Kurdish state. It was the possible conjuncture between Kurdish nationalism and Islamism, the bugaboos of the interwar period, that most frightened Ankara. Turkey's policy toward the Iranian revolution was to prevent either of these two threats from infecting the body politic of Turkey. Turkey's policy was therefore one of caution.

Suha Bolukbasi maintains that Ankara's attitude toward the Islamic revolution was driven by three main policies: to coexist with Iran, to maintain strict neutrality in the Iran-Iraq war, and take advantage of the war to expand its economic ties with Iran. He asserts that Turkey's decision "to cope with Iran was mainly a deliberate attempt to prevent Tehran from falling into the Soviet sphere of influence."[41] He adds that the U.S. administration did not raise any objections to this policy. There is no doubt that neither Turkey nor the U.S. wanted Iran to fall into the Soviet orbit, but given the fact that less than a decade later the Soviet Union itself collapsed, it must have been understood in Ankara that the Soviet Union would not be able to devour Iran no matter how much Turkey depended on CIA prognostications about the continuing strength of the Soviet Union.

The two primary concerns of Turkey were exacerbated further by Iraq's invasion of Iran on 22 September 1980. Just ten days before the invasion, there was a military coup in Turkey. One of the major reasons

---

[41]Suha Bolukbasi, "Turkey Copes with Revolutionary Iran," *Journal of South Asian and Middle Eastern Studies*, vol. xiii, no. 1 & 2 (1989):95.

for the military again assuming power in Turkey was the generals' growing concerns with alliances between various leftist Turkish and Kurdish nationalist groups. It is likely that the Turkish government and the TAF knew of the intended Iraqi attack on Iran. Given the turbulent political scene in Turkey, the TAF undoubtedly wished to take the precaution of having military rule and martial law in place throughout the Kurdish provinces to ensure against unrest. Military rule in Turkey from 1980 to 1983 also increased the state's capacity to squash the domestic Islamist movements as well as the PKK movement within Turkey and to counter the pro-Islamist propaganda emanating from Tehran.

Another major factor that induced Turkey to coexist with Iran and its revolution, especially after the outbreak of the Iran-Iraq war, was the opportunity that it allowed for increased trade with both belligerents. After the military came to power in 1980, it was decided that Turkey would embark on a liberalization of its economy, including more privatization and developing an export-oriented economy. Such a policy demanded the accumulation of capital and Ankara determined that one of the sources of the needed capital could be Iran. Trade between the two countries rose from less than $1 billion in 1980 to $2.5 billion by 1985, although subsequently it declined.[42]

During periods when states are energetically trying to accumulate capital for industrialization purposes, they tend to be cautious about getting involved in external wars unless the regime and its leadership feels threatened. This is explicit in the omni-balancing paradigm offered at the beginning of the this book. Fred Lawson has argued recently that Syria did not go to war with Turkey in the 1990s because of Syria's need to accumulate capital and to protect its economic strategy, in spite of severely strained relations between the two countries resulting from disputes over the allocations of Euphrates river water and Damascus' support and headquartering of the PKK and its leader, Abdullah Öcalan.[43]

A similar argument is applicable to Turkey. Its desire to accumulate capital was greater than any perceived threat that Iran offered. It would have been much easier for Turkey to find reasons to go to war with Syria

---

[42]Bolukbasi, 100.

[43] Fred H. Lawson, *Why Syria Goes to War: Thirty Years of Confrontation* (Ithaca: Cornell University Press, 1996), 129-156. On the Syria-Turkish relations see Robert Olson, "Turkey-Syria Relations Since the Gulf War: Kurds and Water," *Middle East Policy*, vol. v, no. 2 (1997):168-93.

in the 1980s and 1990s than with Iran. Some of the economic factors inhibiting Syria's desire for war with Turkey were reciprocated by Turkey. Many of the same demands for capital accumulation played a role in Turkey's policy of coexistence with Iran. In my view these needs persisted through the 1990s. While Iran's need for capital accumulation was great, it was obviously not the prime consideration of the Iranian regime during the early years of the Islamic revolution.[44] The driving force of Iran's policy during this time was to obtain legitimacy for the regime, defeat Iraq and lessen its isolation in regional and world politics. But it can be argued that after 1989 the need for capital accumulation also played a moderating role in Iran's relations with its neighbors, especially large non-Arab countries such as Turkey.

The major factor that could have contributed to upsetting Turkey-Iran relations was the Kurdish question and the two countries' Kurdish problems. The focus of tension regarding the Kurdish question was not either country's policies toward the Kurds in their respective countries, but their efforts to dominate the Kurds in northern Iraq after Baghdad's diminishing influence in that region as the Iran-Iraq war continued. The major Turkish concern was that Baghdad was no longer able to control northern Iraq and that the KDP and/or the PUK would cooperate with the PKK, which had ensconced itself in northern Iraq and northern Iran in the early years of the war. Ankara had cause for concern, since in July 1983 the KDP and PKK had signed an accord called "Principles of Solidarity" in which they agreed to cooperate against their common enemies.[45] Their pact did not last long and the two groups were soon at loggerheads. After the Persian Gulf war the two groups clashed continually.

Even before the PKK-KDP accord, Ankara had become worried, and on 26 May 1983, Turkey attacked the PKK in northern Iraq with from 8,000 to 10,000 troops, penetrating up to 25 miles into Iraq and capturing several hundred PKK members.[46] It was Baghdad's approval of the attack

---

[44]Anoushiravan Etheshami, *After Khomeini: The Iranian Second Republic* (London: Routledge, 1995), 27-125.

[45]Michael Gunter, "Kurdish Infighting: The PKK-KDP Conflict," in *The Kurdish Nationalist Movement in the 1990s: Its Impact on Turkey and the Middle East*, ed. Robert Olson (Lexington, KY: University Press of Kentucky, 1996), 51-2 and ff.

[46]I have no intention here of getting into the numbers game. It is reasonable to assume that not as many PKK were killed as Ankara claimed. It seems possible

that irritated Tehran. Iran's constant mantra against Turkey was that it was helping Iraq protect its oil regions in the interests of NATO and the U.S. interests. When Baghdad acquiesced to Turkey's demands for a "hot-pursuit" treaty in October 1984, Tehran refused a similar request by the Turks. The Iranians agreed, however, to a "security agreement" on 28 November 1984 requiring "each country to prohibit any activity on its territory aimed against the other's security."[47] For Turkey the threat was obviously the PKK; for Iran it was the oppositional movements in Turkey, especially the *mojahedin-i halq*. By 1989 there were also between 1 and 1.5 million Iranians in Turkey whose political activities worried Iran. The 1984 security accord did not apply to Iraq and both countries presumably felt free to support each other's enemies.

On 15 August 1986 Turkey made another incursion into northern Iraq against the PKK. More incursions followed on 3-4 and 27 March 1987. Majlis Speaker Hashemi Rafsanjani accused Ankara of planning to seize the Kirkuk oil field. This was an accusation that Tehran continued to levy throughout the 1990s. While one of Tehran's persistent charges against Turkey has been that it wanted to control the oil fields of northern Iraq, it seems doubtful that this was or is Turkey's primary objective. Controlling the oil fields of northern Iraq would mean controlling, at least partially, the 3.5 million Kurds in northern Iraq. Fred Halliday has asserted there is only 20 years' worth of oil left in the northern Iraq fields.[48] Graham Fuller on the other hand thinks that oil is still an important factor, as 1.5 million barrels a year were still being produced in 1990.[49] Nader Entessar also stresses that Tehran "is fearful that Turkey will seek either directly or indirectly to control the oil fields of northern Iraq, thus altering the balance of power in the region."[50] Henri Barkey, who has written

---

that non-PKK were included in the body counts as well.

[47]Bolukbasi, 103-4.

[48]Fred Halliday, "The Gulf War and Its Aftermath: First Impressions," *International Affairs*, vol. 67, no. 2 (1991):232. Halliday provides no sources for his declaration.

[49]Graham E. Fuller, "Turkey's New Eastern Orientation," in *Turkey's New Geopolitics: From the Balkans to Western China*, ed. Graham E. Fuller and Ian O. Lesser (Boulder: Westview Press, 1993), 60.

[50]Nader Entessar, "Kurdish Conflict in Regional Perspective," in *Change and*

extensively on Turkey's Kurdish problem, agrees with Halliday that oil is not the prime concern of Turkey's policy in northern Iraq and that Ankara's policy is "driven by one goal: to eliminate any influence that encourages Turkey's Kurds to seek autonomy or independence...Ankara fears that the creation of an independent Kurdish state or even a federated entity within a reconstituted Iraq would fuel the fires of autonomy in Turkey. Turkey's preoccupation with the Kurds eclipses all of its other regional concerns, including the potential danger that an Iraq, ruled by an erratic regime armed to the teeth, possibly with nuclear weapons, in control of 20% of the world's known oil reserves, could pose to Turkey's security."[51]

It is difficult to predict a Turkish or Iranian policy toward the Kurds in northern Iraq based on speculation as to how much oil reserves remain in the northern Iraqi fields, especially when it enters the argument from an undocumented source. Barkey wrote his analysis in 1993 and some five years later it still has strong support. I argue that Turkey's control, especially via military occupation of northern Iraq, has been and is Iran's primary concern regarding growing Turkish influence in northern Iraq, as seems to be the case in the 1990s as it was in the 1980s, Tehran's fear is that Turkish control, even political control of northern Iraq, such as over the KDP, would move Turkey's security border a few hundred miles to the south and east. This movement eastward of Turkey's *de facto* national security perimeter worries Tehran. Such a movement would mean that a direct Turkish influenced region in northern Iraq would abut the Kurdish-Azeri populated region for 200 or more miles. The Azeri population of Iran is generally estimated to be around 10 million or 16.5 percent of Iran's population of some 60 million in 1997. It is speculuated that Azeris also comprise 75 percent of the *bazaari*s in Tehran and are influential in many sectors of Iranian society. As mentioned earlier, the greatest challenge to Iran's territorial integrity after its independence in 1925 came in 1946 with the establishment of the Kurdish Mahabad Republic and the Democratic Republic of Azerbaijan: a heady reminder of Azeri and Kurdish nationalism. It seems unlikely that any Iranian government would want to repeat that experience.

Continuity in the Middle East: Conflict Resolution and Prospects for Peace, ed. M. E. Ahrari (New York: St. Martin's Press, 1996), 66.

[51]Henri J. Barkey, "Turkey's Kurdish Dilemma," *Survival,* vol. 35, no. 4 (1993):64.

The collapse of the Soviet Union and the independence of Azerbaijan in 1991 increased immediately Iran's fears that the aroused nationalism of the new republic, filled with Turkic nationalist symbols, would spill over into and affect its own Azeri population. The Islamic legitimated regime in Tehran, with all of the problems it was confronting, certainly did not desire to have Azerbaijan nationalism affect its own Azeri population, especially in its northern provinces, incidentally called East and West Azerbaijan. If Turkey had its Kurdish problem, Iran had a potential Azeri problem after 1991. Most of all, Tehran did not want to be confronted with a simultaneous Azeri-Kurdish problem encompassing some 21 million people-10 million Azeris in Iran, 5 million in the Azerbaijan Republic and 6 million Kurds in Iran. Tehran's policy toward Azerbaijan after 1991 and toward the Caucasus, including the Armenian-Azerbaijan conflict over Norgorno-Karabagh, was geared to prevent Azerbaijani nationalism from affecting its own Azeri population. This, more than trying to counter Turkey's attempts to gather more influence in Azerbaijan itself, seems to have been Iran's primary objective.

Good evidence of Iran's concern regarding the Azeri question is that in April 1993 it made Ardabil, a city in northeastern Iran, a province in its own right. Previously it had been a lesser district within the province of East Azerbaijan with its capital city of Tabriz. One of the reasons for elevating the status of Ardabil was to lessen the attraction of the Republic of Azerbaijan's nationalist rhetoric.[52]

Tehran was also no doubt concerned, especially from 1988 onward, about the exploitation and distribution of the oil and natural gas resources in the Caspian Sea region. By July 1997, American officials estimated Caspian Sea oil resources of 250 billion barrels, with Azerbaijan having an estimated 32 billion barrels. The immense natural gas reserves in the region, especially in Turkmenistan and Kazakhstan, required that Iran adopt policies that would allow the country to share and participate as fully as possible in the exploitation of these resources.[53]

The high figures for the oil reserves of Azerbaijan were supplied by U.S. Undersecretary of State Strobe Talbot during President of Azerbaijan Haidar Aliyev's early August visit to Washington. Dilip Hiro

---

[52]H.E. Chehabi, "Ardabil Becomes a Province: Center-Periphery Relations in Iran," *International Journal of Middle East Studies*, vol. 29, no. 2 (1997):235-53.

[53]For these and other concerns see Fuller, 37-98.

thinks the reason for the inflated estimates of the Caspian Sea Basin oil reserves is that the U.S. government wants to reassure Americans that there are large supplies of oil outside the Persian Gulf region. If Persian Gulf oil is cut off, there is more around the Caspian Sea. He also speculates that "creating a hoopla about the increasing oil bonanza in the Caspian Sea makes the oil-rich Arab states nervous and helps to keep the price of oil low."[54] The *British Petroleum Statistical Review of World Energy Sources* states that at the end of 1996, Azerbaijan's proven oil reserves were 7 billion barrels, i.e., four and a half times less than the American figure.

Many of the various pipeline schemes to transport the oil and the gas from the Caspian Sea basin to markets in Russia, Europe and the U.S. are still in the process of negotiation. Iran wants some of the pipelines to traverse its territory whether or not they carry Iranian oil or gas, and it seems likely that if pipelines do cross Iranian territory they will, at some point, carry Iran's oil and gas. Some of the planned pipelines crossing northern Iran and Turkey would have to cross territories heavily Kurdish and areas in Turkey where the PKK has been active for 15 years. This would mean even closer Turkish and Iranian security cooperation against the possibility of Kurdish sabotage.[55]

Iran, Turkey and Turkmenistan announced in May 1997 that a gas pipeline from western Turkmenistan would pass 1,250 kilometers through Iran to Turkey and terminate some 100 kilometers later in Van, a province in eastern Turkey. The Turkmenistan-Iran connection is finished. Most of the distance in Iran is already covered by an existing pipeline and the spur to Van is under construction and is scheduled for completion in late 1998.

As mentioned above, some portions of the pipeline in Iran and the connector from Iran to Van pass through territories inhabited heavily by Kurds. In addition there has been major fighting between the PKK and the TAF in the area of the pipeline in Turkey for more than a decade. The

---

[54]Dilip Hiro, "Why is the U.S. Inflating Caspian Sea Reserves?" *Middle East International*, no. 558 (12 September 1997):18-19.

[55]There was a plethora of reports in the news media in August 1997 during President of Azerbaijan Haidar Aliyev's visit to Washington. While in Washington Aliyev announced several billion dollars' worth of deals for the exploitation of Azerbaijan's oil and gas with American and European companies.

completion of the Turkmenistan-Iran-Turkey gas pipeline would lessen the reliance of Turkey on the proposed Baku-Tbilisi-Supsa-Ceyhan oil pipeline that is also almost completed, with the exception of the portion from Georgia to Ceyhan. Moscow has stated that the Georgia to Ceyhan portion of the pipeline "will never take off" as it would have to cross areas of Kurdistan where PKK fighters have been waging war against Ankara for 15 years. Mahir Valat, the PKK representative to the Commonwealth of Independent States (CIS) and eastern Europe stated that for "the pipeline to pass areas controlled by the PKK one would need to exterminate the PKK."[56] Ankara's intention of course is to do just that. Turkey's view is that if Iran wants to participate in the growing network of oil and gas pipelines disseminating from the Caspian Sea region, it should help Turkey to exterminate the PKK or, at least, expel them from Iranian territories.

In short, toward the end of the 1990s, the saliency of the Kurdish question as a factor in Turkish-Iranian relations is diminishing because of the need of both countries to develop their economies. Turkey's energy needs will increase by one-third in the next decade. Iran, possessing large oil reserves and some of the largest deposits of natural gas in the world—second only to Russia's holdings—needs to market that oil and gas. Tehran's greater participation in the exploitation and distribution of these energy sources will also contribute to the lessening of its diplomatic and economic isolation.

There are other factors that impel Turkey and Iran to cooperate not only on the Kurdish question but also on a host of other issues, despite their competition in Central Asia and in the Caucasus. Both countries will have a population of around 70 million by the year 2,000; they have the strongest agriculture base in the Middle East, the most arable land and, with the exception of Israel, the most diverse and highly developed economies, not based on oil (although Iran's economy is still heavily dependent on oil). In 1997 Turkey had a GNP of over $200 billion, and Iran had one of $90 billion. Turkey expected to increase its exports by the year 2,000 to $50 billion from its current $33 billion. Iran with its oil and tremendous gas reserves has the potential to increase its GDP rapidly in the next two decades. Barring destruction or severe crippling either militarily or economically by Europe or the U.S. and, again with the

---

[56]*TRKNWS-L* (an internet Turkish news service), 19 December 1996 from the newspaper *Kommersant* written by Georgili Dvali and Andrea Smirov.

exception of Israel, recognizing that the U.S. occupies the Arab portion of the Perisan Gulf, both Turkey and Iran are fast becoming the most important countries in the Middle East. Indeed, during the first quarter of the 21st century we may see an even further increase in the influence of Iran and Turkey to the levels attained during the first part of the eighteenth century before Europe began to whittle away the power of the Ottoman and Qajar empires. The influence the Arab countries gained in the twentieth century will be diminished in the twentieth-first century. The main significance of the Arab countries situated around the Persian Gulf will be to supply energy to the world. Both Turkey and Iran have the hinterlands of Central Asia in which to participate; both are in a strong position to have good trading relations with Russia as well as with Europe and Asia.

While neither country may achieve all that it wants in mutually competing economic spheres, it seems unlikely that either would allow the Kurds, either internally or in Iraq, and in the case of Turkey, in Syria, to jeopardize their economic strategies or hopes. Turkey has made this clear by its war against the PKK in Turkey and in northern Iraq. By 1993 Ankara was estimated already to be spending $8 billion a year in its war against the PKK, a sum that rose considerably after its large incursions in 1995 and 1997. The cost overruns of the 1997 campaign became a issue between the WP government and the TAF before Erbakan was ousted from office on 18 June.[57] The evacuation, flight and ethnic cleansing of some 3 million Kurds in southeastern and eastern Turkey and the TAF's destruction of some 3,600 villages and hamlets attests to the desire of the TAF to exterminate the PKK and to crush militant Kurdish nationalism.

Indeed, one has to consider whether the policies of the Turkish government, especially after 1991, were meant not only to ensure that Turkey's Kurds would not seek autonomy or independence but were also to make southeastern and eastern Turkey safe for the passages of oil and gas pipelines coming from the Caspian Sea basin and Central Asia. After the devastation wreaked in the region during the past decade, Kurds will enjoy little of the economic development that will occur in the region. The same could be said of the Southeast Anatolia Project popularly known under its acronym GAP (Güneydoğu Projesi), the $50 billion hydroelectric, irrigation and tourism project in southeastern Turkey.[58]

---

[57]Barkey, 58-60.

[58]For more on the GAP see Robert Olson, "Turkey-Syria Relations," 190-1 and

Whether the GAP achieves all that is hoped for it, it is clear that Kurds will receive little from the project. Indeed, if the staggering amount of immigration of Kurds to the western provinces continues, there may be few Kurds left in the area to benefit from the economic developments now occurring and projected to take place in the future with the exception of large land owners and small numbers of entrepreneurs. The reduction of the Kurdish population in the GAP region reduces the chances for the PKK and/or other Kurdish nationalist or disgruntled groups from sabotaging the GAP installations. The emigration of the Kurds also makes the GAP region more attractive to foreign investors, including, as we shall see later, Israel. Tel Aviv wants access to the waters of the Euphrates and the Ceyhan and Seyhan rivers and reservoirs that are part of the GAP project. This is a policy supported strongly by the U.S. and Europe, who believe that such access is necessary to provide the future water needs of Israel and its Arab dependencies. This explains in part the series of military, economic and trading agreements that Israel and Turkey signed from 1995 onward. The Ankara-Tel Aviv agreements also put pressure on Syria to stop sheltering Abdullah Öcalan, the leader of the PKK.[59]

The Turkey-Israel agreements did not directly affect Turkey-Iran relations with regard to the Kurdish question. Tehran was concerned, however, that strong pressures on Syria to stop sheltering and aiding the PKK would weaken its major ally in the Middle East—weaken its ability to resist Israel and U.S. dictates in the "peace process" and diminish Damascus' ability to support the PKK and/or the PUK in northern Iraq, especially the former after full scale war broke out between the PKK and

---

accompanying notes; Carl E. Nestor, "Dimensions of Turkey's Kurdish Question and the Potential Impact of the Southeast Anatolian Project (GAP): Part I, *The International Journal of Kurdish Studies*, vol. 8, no. 1 & 2 (1995):33-78; Part II, vol. 9, no. 1 & 2 (1995):35-78; Servet Mutlu, "The Southeastern Anatolia Project (GAP) of Turkey: Its Context, Objectives and Prospects," *Orient*, vol. 37, no. 1 (1996):59-86. Mutlu's caution on the GAP is based on his view that the funds allocated for development of irrigated agriculture may not be sufficient and that the agricultural extension and training system is inadequate. A host of other problems, including attracting appropriate industrial capital and personnel, according to Mutlu, "will make long-term sustainable development difficult if not impossible" (81).

[59]*Ibid.*

the KDP in 1992. Tehran found Damascus' support for the PKK useful in its own efforts to expand its sphere of influence in northern Iraq against the KDP. Tehran's support of the PKK both in northern Iraq and in Iran itself became stronger after the KDP tightened its alliance with Ankara in 1992.

There are then three major geostrategical and geopolitical concerns that require Turkey's and Iran's cooperation for the management of the Kurdish question: 1) their mutual interest in participating in the oil and gas resources and their distributive networks; 2) their desire to refrain from undue interference in each other's policies in the Caucasus and Central Asia, especially with regard to Azerbaijan and the accompanying Azeri question in Iran and; 3) their need to agree on their respective spheres of influence in northern Iraq. The last concern dictates that Turkey not establish a sphere of control close to the Iraq-Iran border and further that Turkey not try to play the "Azeri card" through its actions or proxies in northern Iraq. In turn Ankara expects Tehran not to support policies that would lead to a strong Kurdish autonomy in northern Iraq and so encourage the Kurds in Turkey to do the same. Tehran, too, does not want to see Turkish control over the oil and gas pipelines in northern Iraq or Turkish influence on Kurdish groups such as the Kurdistan Democratic Party of Iran (KDPI) in northern Iran. Tehran would rather have Baghdad control the pipelines and the oil than Ankara. Ankara and Baghdad signed a $2.5 billion gas agreement in May 1997, an agreement that is bound eventually to limit further the jurisdiction of the KDP and PUK. By mid 1997 Turkey and Iran seemed to have reached a tacit understanding regarding their sphere of influence in northern Iraq: Turkey was allied with the KDP and Iran with the PUK. During fighting of the two Kurdish groups after the Turkish incursion in the spring and summer of 1997, the KDP fought with the Turks; the PUK abstained at first, then fought with the PKK; both groups were supported by Iran. It could well be that a tacit understanding between Ankara and Tehran may well act as a restraint on the maximal objectives of each Kurdish group. This is a situation that could lead Baghdad to assert itself more strongly in the north. But as Iraq attempts to regain more control over the north of the country, it will have to negotiate its progress with Ankara and Tehran, which adds another level of management to the Kurdish question.

I shall attempt to show in the remainder of this essay that after the Persian Gulf war in 1991 neither Turkey nor Iran allowed the Kurdish question in all of its manifestations to endanger their own interests discussed above. The major disruption in the two countries' relations resulted not from the differences over the Kurdish question but from alleged Iranian support for the Islamist movement in Turkey, especially the WP, in the aftermath of which both countries expelled their counterparts' ambassadors and other diplomatic personnel.

CHAPTER FOUR

The Kurdish Question after the Persian Gulf War

The major problem between Ankara and Tehran regarding the Kurdish question resulted from Turkey's major campaigns in 1992, 1995 and 1997 into northern Iraq. The number of troops involved in these incursions grew in size from 10,000 in 1992 to 50,000 to 60,000 in 1997. Iran's response to the 1992 incursion was muted, but Tehran was suspicious of Turkey's intentions as a result of its alliance with the U.S. led Allied forces during the Persian Gulf war. Both countries had a mutual interest in avoiding a large influx of Kurds on their borders. Neither capital wanted the Kurds to become so weak that Saddam Hussein would be able to manipulate them to his advantage. Iran did not want Barzani or Talabani to use their forces in collaboration with the Shi'is during their rebellion after the war. Tehran also would have liked the Kurds to help it oust the *mojahedin-i halq* from its bases in Iraq.[60] Ankara as always wanted to prevent the Kurdish situation in Iraq from affecting the Kurds in Turkey. For this reason, Ankara supported a "safe haven" for the Kurds in northern Iraq, a proposal that purportedly was first broached by Turkish President Turgut Özal before given currency by Prime Minister John Major of Great Britain.

The Iranians were less sanguine about the safe haven and opposed the military force, Operation Provide Comfort (OPC), that accompanied it. Tehran thought OPC provided yet another entree for the U.S. into the region in addition to its occupation of the Arab countries of the Persian Gulf. OPC provided for a "no-fly zone" for Iraqi fixed-wing aircraft north the of 36th parallel. Iran also feared that the safe haven would become an enclave of anti-Iranian oppositional groups, especially the KDPI. The Iranians thought the U.S. supported attacks from the territory north of the

---

[60]Entessar, "Kurdish Conflict in a Regional Perspective," 62.

36th parallel into Iranian territory. As a result, throughout the spring and summer of 1993, Iran bombed KDPI camps within the no-fly zone. Tehran was further upset by the KDPI's propaganda that stated Ankara's policy toward its Kurds was more benevolent than Tehran's—an absurd comparison given the fact that the Turks were already engaged in ethnic cleansing practices against the Kurds. From 1993 to 1995, it seems that Ankara was willing to use its support of the KDPI as a lever to prevent Iran from supporting the PKK. The record indicates, however, that Iranian aid for the PKK both in northern Iraq and for PKK camps in northern Iran was greater than Turkey's support for the KDPI. Tehran needed to establish a credible plausible deniability from 1993 onward in so far as its support for the PKK was concerned in order that Ankara not give too strong support to Iranian oppositional groups, especially the *mojahedin-i halq* organization, whether in Turkey or in Iraq. From 1992 to 1998 both countries saw it as in their interest to manage the trans-state Kurdish question in northern Iraq in order to lessen its effects on their own Kurdish problems and, in the case of Iran, to deter oppositional groups to the regime. Nader Entessar has argued that the May 1992 elections to establish a regional federal government in northern Iraq, and the possibility that an independent Kurdish state might possibly emerge in the future compelled closer cooperation between the two capitals "while at the same time increasing suspicions about the ultimate goals of each country in its new dealings with the emerging Kurdish state."[61]

The Turkey-Iran Security Protocols to Prevent the Emergence of a Kurdish State

While both Ankara and Tehran had to acquiesce in U.S. and European support for an autonomous entity in northern Iraq, both capitals were in agreement that it was not in their mutual interests to have an independent Kurdish state emerge from such an entity.[62] From 1993 onward both the Turks and Iranians, (along with Syria, the other country in addition to Iraq that did not want to see the emergence of a Kurdish state in northern Iraq) signed a series of security protocols to prevent such from happening. It was easy for Tehran to include Syria in the security protocols as they

---

[61]*Ibid.* 65.

[62]For more on these developments see Michael M. Gunter, "A *de facto* Kurdish State in Northern Iraq," *Third World Quarterly*, vol. 14, no. 2 (1993):295-319.

had a series of alliances and agreements on a broad range of issues going back all the way to the 1980s.[63] Despite the important differences between Ankara and Damascus over aspects of the Kurdish question and water, they joined ranks with Iran to prevent the emergence of a Kurdish state in northern Iraq—something all three countries suspected the U.S. and Europe wanted.

After the Turkish incursion into northern Iraq in March 1992, Ankara and Tehran engaged in what became a series of security protocols with Damascus to prevent the emergence of a Kurdish state in northern Iraq and to restrict Kurdish nationalist movements in the Middle East and Europe that threatened their respective regimes. The security measures called for meetings at the foreign minister level every six months with frequent meetings among lower ranking officials. The first-post 1992 protocol was signed in Ankara on 30 November 1993. It stipulated that neither country would permit any terrorist organization, i.e., the PKK, to exist on its territory. Golam Hosseini Bolandijian of the Iranian delegation, authorized representative of President Rafsanjani, stated that Iran would take measures against the PKK. The 7 December 1993 issue of the Turkish conservative newspaper, *Sabah*, had a banner headline proclaiming, "Iran issues order for PKK members to be shot." Bolandijian reportedly stated, "Iran has issued an order for any PKK member to be shot regardless of whether they are wearing PKK uniforms or are smugglers." The article concluded, "At the end of seven (security) meetings between the Iranian and Turkish delegations a protocol to take action against terrorism was signed."

On 4 May 1994, Turkish Interior Minister Nahit Menteşe announced that Iran had turned over to Turkey 28 members of the PKK, 10 of whom were corpses. On 13 June Ankara requested of visiting Iranian Interior Minister Mohammad Besharati that Turkey be allowed to bomb PKK bases located around the areas of Mt. Ararat and Mt. Tendürek (Lesser Ararat) in and near Iranian territory, the same area in which much fighting had taken place from 1927 to 1930. On 14 June, President Süleyman Demirel even took time out from his summer vacation to announce that Ankara and Tehran had agreed to cooperate against the PKK, and the Turkish press announced on 16 June that Iran had given permission to Turkey to bomb PKK bases located in Iranian territory. The declaration

---

[63]For the reasons and origins of the alliance see Ehteshami and Hinnebusch; the whole book deals with this topic and much more.

centered on three major points of agreement: 1) that PKK members must be prevented from passing from northern Iraq to Iran; 2) that PKK members must be prevented from passing to Armenia and thence to Russia; and 3) Turkey would be allowed to bomb roads in Iranian territory that were used by the PKK to replenish supplies for their camps in Iran from which they launched attacks against Turkey. In a press conference Besharati did not officially acknowledge that Iran would give permission to Turkey to bomb PKK bases located in Iranian territory, but he stated that Iran would cooperate with Turkey in every way against "their common enemies." In return, Ankara announced that it would move "against" the *mojahedin-i halq* opposition based in Turkey. Menteşe proclaimed that Turkey would not allow any group operating from Turkish territory "to give harm" to the Iranian government.

By 1 September 1994 around ten major security meetings among the highest level officials had taken place between Turkey and Iran. The main topic at all of them appears to have been the efforts of each country to control those groups they thought most threatened their regimes.

The national security concerns between the two countries concerning the Kurds specifically were given prominence when President Demirel met with President Rafsanjani in Tehran on 15-17 July 1994; this was the first visit by a Turkish president to Iran in decades and notably dealt with the challenge of the Kurds. In press interviews prior to the meeting, Rafsanjani gave assurances that Iran was fully cooperating with Turkey against the PKK, and he stated that the creation of a Kurdish state was "impossible."[64] Although Rafsanjani did make a point of claiming that the Islamic Republic had solved its Kurdish problem within the "spirit of Islam," this reply was probably meant to imply his approval of the religiously oriented WP in Turkey, which was in opposition to Demirel's True Path Party (TPP). The Demirel-Rafsanjani meeting received wide coverage in both the Iranian and Turkish presses, but it was more limited in Turkey because of the hullabaloo over the disclosure of Prime Minister Tansu Çiller's and her husband's personal wealth and the fact that the couple had some 4 or 5 million dollars invested in real estate in the U.S. Foreign Minister Hikmet Çetin was also forced to resign during Demirel's visit in Tehran. While it is still unclear as to all of the reasons compelling Çetin's resignation, his handling of the Kurdish question and Turkey's Kurdish problem and its many manifestations may well have played a role

---

[64]*Hürriyet*, 22 July 1994

in his forced resignation. Çetin himself is an ethnic Kurd and was perceived by the TAF to be "soft" on the Kurdish issue. Nahit Menteşe, the Turkish interior minister, announced that he was confident the new security agreements between the two countries as well as agreements with Syria would lead to the capture of PKK leader Öcalan, who, like the recently apprehended Carlos the Jackal, "could not escape justice forever."[65]

Turkish and Iranian relations continued to improve in early 1995. Much of the improvement centered on Iran's potential participation in an international consortium of companies to build a natural gas pipeline from Turkmenistan to Turkey discussed above.[66] Immediately in the wake of the natural gas pipeline negotiations, Iran moved to settle a $200 million debt it had with Turkish exporters.[67]

Preventing the emergence of an independent Kurdish state in northern Iraq was again the major topic of discussion by the foreign ministers of Turkey, Iran and Syria during their 7th Tripartite meeting in Tehran on 8 September 1995, the first foreign minister level meeting since the large Turkish incursion into northern Iraq in the spring. The incursion was denounced by Tehran and Damascus as violating the territorial integrity of Iraq and threatening to fragment the country. Despite their denunciations of a few months earlier, the Iranians and Syrians seemed eager to confer with the Turks in September. The three foreign ministers reaffirmed their previous proclamations: 1) that they were opposed to the division of Iraq; 2) that they were against "terrorism," (but they gave no names); and 3) that all three ministers were concerned about the stockpiling of weapons in northern Iraq.[68]

When Iranian Minister of Economic and Financial Affairs Morteza Mohammad Khan met with President Demirel on 7 November 1995 in Ankara, Demirel stated that he fully agreed with the decisions reached at

---

[65]Carlos the Jackal, the pseudonym of Ilich Ramirez Sanchez, a well known terrorist, was delivered to the French government by the government of Sudan on 15 August 1994.

[66]For details of the pipeline deal as it was being discussed in early 1995 see *Hürriyet*, 10 January 1995.

[67]*Hürriyet*, 3 February 1995.

[68]*Ettela'at*, 16 September 1995.

the 7th Tripartite talks held in Tehran. He remarked, "Western countries intended to form a Kurdish state with the help of separatists."[69] He also repeated that Turkey and Iran were not in competition with each other. In turn, Mohammed Khan stressed the need for greater economic cooperation between the two countries. On 1 December Turkish Foreign Ministry Undersecretary Önur Öymen visited Iran and held talks with President Rafsanjani in which the President noted the good relations between Tehran and Ankara, but he, too, indicated Iran's desire for more economic cooperation.

The national security agreements between Turkey and Iran after the Persian Gulf war and through 1995 were important in several ways: 1) they indicated the serious challenge of Kurdish nationalism to both countries, especially of the PKK to Turkey; 2) they suggested that Ankara and Tehran were more willing than previously thought, especially in the West, to cooperate regarding their respective policies toward countries in the Caucasus, especially with regard to Armenia and Azerbaijan and the accompanying problem of Norgorno-Karabagh and, by extension, the increasingly strong role and presence of Russia in the region; 3) they indicated that the two countries were prepared to be more cooperative in their policies toward the Central Asian states; and 4) they acknowledged the need for Turkey to maintain close coordination with Iran in order to prevent the emergence of an independent Kurdish state in northern Iraq that would be a dagger aimed at the bosom of each country bringing geopolitical and geostrategical headaches to the two capitals.

From the Persian Gulf war to the end of 1995, Turkey-Iran relations regarding the Kurdish question went through many fluctuations. In spite of the cooperation evinced by the numerous Tripartite meetings, the emergence of areas in northern Iraq no longer under the control of Baghdad meant necessarily greater competition between Ankara and Tehran for and in that space. The problem was and remains the question of where the lines of the two countries' spheres of influence are to be drawn. This problem was exacerbated in 1994 and 1995 as the two largest Kurdish nationalist groups in northern Iraq, the KDP and PUK drew closer respectively, to Turkey and Iran as the result of their internecine fighting.

An example of the creation of spheres of influence in Iraqi Kurdistan was the reported agreement of Jalal Talabani to allow the existence of

---

[69]*Ettela'at*, 10 November 1995.

3,000 to 5,000 troops, consisting of Shi'is who had earlier fled Iraq and were now under the control of Ayatollah Bakr al-Hakim, a member of the Supreme Assembly for the Islamic Revolution in Iraq (SAIRI).[70] Talabani announced that the force would be used in joint operations with his *peshmergas* (soldiers) against Saddam Husayn. Safa'in Diza'i, the KDP's representative in Ankara, emphasized that the KDP had nothing to do with the deployment and that it was entirely Talabani's decision. He noted further that the KDP was following closely developments in the PUK-controlled region, that by the end of 1995 included half of the territory of northern Iraq and 70 percent of the region's population. Diza'i said the decision to deploy troops in northern Iraq under Iranian control should have been a decision of the Iraqi National Congress (INC) and not solely that of the PUK. Talabani's decision to deploy troops under Iranian control seems to have been made to underline his unhappiness that the PUK was not receiving its fair share of the taxes on trucks carrying food from Turkey and oil from Iraq back to Turkey. In 1995 the taxes and revenues may already have been around $200,000 to $300,000 per day or even higher. The Khabur/Habur crossing point between Turkey and Iraq was under the control of the KDP, which was now in close alliance with Ankara. As the KDP grew more economically dependent on Turkey, the PUK had to open its borders wider to Iranian trade, and one of the demands of Tehran was greater presence in northern Iraq in order to counter that of Turkey. By the end of 1995 each Kurdish organization was becoming the proxy of its big neighbor benefactor.

Aziz Qader, the leader of the 250,000 Turkomen in northern Iraq, claimed that the Shi'a force was paid for entirely by Iran and that Talabani requested the force as a result of the increasingly close relations between the KDP and Turkey, a development feared equally by the PUK and Tehran. PUK and Tehran fears increased after the PKK attacked the KDP in August 1995 and the KDP was compelled to coordinate many of its military operations against the PKK with the TAF.

The deployment of troops ostensibly under the control of an Iranian Ayatollah in PUK-controlled territory of northern Iraq indicated a further diminution of the agreements reached at the Drogheda Conferences in Ireland in August and September 1995. The major result of the first conference was that the PKK used it as a reason to attack the KDP. Abdullah Öcalan characterized Ma'sud Barzani and the KDP as puppets

---

[70]*Hürriyet*, 3 November 1995; *Iran Times*, 3 December 1995.

of the U.S. and Turkey. Öcalan was also apparently impatient to test the unhappiness of some of the Kurds in Bahdinan, the KDP controlled area of northern Iraq, to learn if they were as unhappy with Barzani as the PKK leader thought. The PUK was also unhappy with other aspects of the Drogheda Conference, and it did not come to the aid of the KDP when it was attacked by PKK forces on 25 August. By the end of 1995 the jostling between Ankara and Tehran had resulted in a situation in northern Iraq in which KDP-controllled territory was being brought under a Turkish-controlled economic and political sphere of influence punctuated with intermittent large military incursions in which the KDP and the TAF were allied against the PKK. The PUK-controlled territory was becoming more economically and politically aligned with Iran. In order to maintain its broader geopolitical cooperation with Iran, Turkey was compelled to accept the failure of the Drogheda Conferences, which had excluded Iran, and allow it a greater sphere of influence in northern Iraq. In other words, Ankara's geopolitical need to contain the PKK compelled it to cooperate with Iran and thus allowed Iran to put a dent in the "dual containment" policy that the U.S. was implementing to restrain it. This is a good example of the geopolitical needs of middle level regional powers, in this case Turkey, to cooperate with a regional competitor against the geostrategical policies of its superpower ally, the U.S. Turkey's need to violate its alliance with the U.S. was compelled by the threat of the PKK and Kurdish nationalism, which Iran, rather than the U.S., could best help it to contain.

CHAPTER FIVE

The Islamist Movement in Turkey and the Kurdish Question

One reason Turkey sought to manage the Kurdish question and not interfere with Iran's Kurdish problem or to incite Azeri nationalism was its own growing Islamist movement. By 1991, the TAF was concerned about possible Islamist and PKK cooperation. This in turn opened another tense period in relations between the two countries.

An example of the growing tension between the Islamists—those groups in Turkey who advocated more of an Islamist presence in Turkish society, especially in the schools, and the right to wear Islamist attire (a head scarf and long raincoat for women and loose trousers, beards and skull caps for men)—occurred when Uğur Mumcu, a leading writer, journalist and avowed secularist was murdered on 24 January 1993. His murder was allegedly carried out by a right wing Islamist organization, although as of the end of 1997 the culprits had still not been found. The allegations were sufficient to cause a series of demonstrations by secularists opposed to Islamists making inroads into Turkish civil society. After Mumcu's death, secularist groups in Turkey began to stage periodic candlelight vigils during which they blew out the candles declaring, "One minute of darkness for continued enlightenment."[71]

At Mumcu's funeral protestors shouted, "Turkey will not be Iran," "Mullahs out," and "Down with the *Shari'a*." The Turks did not rule out an Iranian connection to Mumcu's death, but President Demirel stated, "We must be very careful and have very accurate information before attributing any blame to Iran as a state." The spokesman for the Iranian Embassy was quick to deny any Iranian involvement in the murder; however, the *mojahedin-i halq* members living in Turkey proclaimed that

---

[71]This account of Mumcu's murder is from Hugh Pope, "Pointing Fingers at Iran,"*Middle East International*, no. 443, 5 February 1993.

Tehran was probably involved in the murder as it had carried out 50 assassinations in Turkey alone, not to mention numerous killings elsewhere, especially in Europe, where the *mojahedin-i halq* charged that Tehran had ordered the assassinations of Abdulrahman Qassemlou, the KDPI leader, (in Vienna in 1989) and that of his successor Sadegh Sharafkanki (in Berlin in 1992). Ankara's fears of the Islamist movement increased when its banner party, the WP, increased its strength in the local elections in 1994, in which they captured the mayorships of a score of cities in Turkey including Ankara and Istanbul.

In February 1993, just a few weeks after Mumcu's death, relations between the two countries took another nose-dive when Turkish police arrested nineteen Turkish Islamist radicals whose papers showed repeated travel to Iran as well as ties to Iran's security forces as far back as the 1970s.[72] During the same month the body of a member of the *mojahedin-i halq* was found and evidence pointed to his torture and death by strangulation after his abduction in Istanbul in 1992. In what was already a common practice regarding alleged Iranian support for the PKK, the Turkish foreign minister handed files of "terrorists" over to the Iranian foreign minister, who in turn denied any Iranian involvement. Prime Minister Demirel insisted, no doubt for geopolitical reasons, that the most important thing was to maintain stability. The Tripartite security meetings to prevent the emergence of a Kurdish state in northern Iraq and to restrain Kurdish nationalism in general continued to take precedence over Iran's alleged support for Islamist groups in Turkey. Another semi-annual Tripartite security meeting took place as scheduled in Damascus on 10 February.

As the two capitals tried to reestablish equilibrium, Ankara nevertheless did nothing to curb the secularist demonstrations against the Islamists. Aziz Nesin, a popular satirical writer in Turkey, vowed to translate Salman Rushdie's *Satanic Verses* into Turkish, and he did publish some excerpts. In Iran, the radical newspaper, *Islamic Republic*, demanded a *fatwa*, a religious decree, ordering Nesin's death just as Ayatollah Khomeini had ordered against Rushdie in 1989. However, Iran, now under the more moderate leadership of Hashemi Rafsanjani, who had become President of Iran in 1989, was not eager for another Rushdie affair, this time with Turkey. The ayatollahs issued no such *fatwa* against

---

[72]Hugh Pope, "Conflict over Killing," *Middle East International*, no. 444, 19 February 1993, 11-2.

50   *The Islamic Movement in Turkey*

Nesin. Nesin died of natural causes in 1996.

In August 1994 tensions rose once more when Ankara charged Iran again with meddling in its internal affairs with accusations that it was supporting the PKK. A Turkish delegation flew to Tehran with a dossier chock-full documenting evidence of "terrorist" activities in and against Turkey by the PKK, carried out with Iran's support. The Turks had photographs, cassette tapes and "files containing revelations by captured PKK militants on PKK ties with Iran's intelligence and *Pasdaran* (revolutionary guards) units, as well as data on the locations of PKK arms depots, training centers, liaison offices, and the names of PKK members who were in charge of the camps and cell houses in Iran."[73]

In June 1995, Ankara charged that Iran permitted the PKK to establish more bases in northern Iran after they had fled from the 35,000 troop strong Turkish spring incursion. According to Ertuğrul Özkök, the managing editor of the pro-government and pro-TAF *Hürriyet* newspaper, the Turks did not take any military action because "attacking a camp in Iran would be a very risky and dangerous initiative. Bombing Iran is quite different from bombing northern Iraq."[74]

Throughout the rest of 1995 tensions between the two capitals remained high largely because of Turkey's belief that Tehran was allowing the PKK to consolidate its activities in northern Iran and that it continued to encourage Islamist elements within Turkey. Iran kept to its stance of maintaining plausible deniability in both instances. On the other hand Tehran was concerned about the consolidation of the relationship between Ankara and the KDP in northern Iraq after Turkey's large scale March incursion. This concern, as mentioned above, impelled Tehran to undermine the arrangements reached in the fall of 1995 at the Drogeda Conferences that had excluded it from participating in its governance.

Iran, however, did not want to increase tensions with Ankara because on 24 December 1995 in the parliamentary elections in Turkey the WP, led by Necmettin Erbakan, had garnered the largest percentage of the vote, 21.3 percent. In June 1996, after long negotiations, the WP was able to form a government in coalition with the TPP, led by Tansu Çiller, who became foreign minister in the new government. Tehran looked upon Erbakan very favorably for several reasons. He was well known to

---

[73]Michael M. Gunter, "The Kurds and the Future of Turkey," (New York: St. Martin's Press, 1997), 95.

[74]*Ibid.* 96; *Hürriyet*, 10 June 1995.

Iranian officials. He had been and continued to be an ardent supporter and admirer of the Islamic regime in Iran; he did not favor the U.S., Tehran's arch enemy; he was an advocate of the D-8, an economic grouping of eight Islamic countries—Turkey, Iran, Pakistan, Bangladesh, Nigeria, Malaysia, Indonesia and Egypt—that would be able to provide a partial alternative to those countries' economic and trading dependence on the European Union (EU), U.S. and Japanese trading blocs. Even more to Tehran's liking was Erbakan's statement immediately after coming to power that in his view neither Iran nor Syria supported the PKK. He rejected such charges as propaganda put out by the CIA to thwart the development of good relations between Islamic countries.

Erbakan made good on his promise to establish better relations with Tehran both for trade and to gain cooperation to crush the PKK. Less than six weeks after assuming office he visited Iran on 10-11 August 1996, his first foreign visit to any country. In spite of Erbakan's expressed goodwill toward Iran, the Turkish media, no doubt with stories planted by the TAF, apprehensive of Erbakan's policies, took the occasion to air their concerns about relations with their big neighbor to the south.

The press in both Turkey and Iran as well as the international press gave prominent coverage to the two countries signing a $23 billion natural gas deal in spite of recent U.S. Congressional legislation calling for sanctions of those companies investing more than $40 million in the gas and oil industries of Iran. However, Turkish and Iranian newspaper accounts of the visit indicate that it was the Kurdish question, i.e., the PKK, that dominated the talks between Rafsanjani and Erbakan, including interestingly, two talks with no one else but their translators present.

The pivotal role that Tehran had come to play in northern Iraq after the failure of the U.S.-backed Drogheda Conference in 1995 was amply demonstrated by the Iranian miliTary thrust of some 90 kilometers into northern Iraq just one week before Erbakan's visit. Prior to his departure, Erbakan and his lieutenants stated that only four countries—Turkey, Iran, Iraq, Syria—where the vast majority of Kurds lived, could "solve" the Kurdish question. Ankara's position, at least the WP's position, was that the Kurdish question had to be solved before a host of other issues among the four countries could be tackled.

Just before Erbakan left for Tehran, the Turkish press aired some of Turkey's concerns in its relations with Tehran, many of which directly or indirectly, were/are affected by the Kurdish question.[75] First was Ankara's

---

[75]*Hürriyet*, 10 August 1996.

worry that Tehran's policy was to prevent Turkey from becoming a major transit route and terminal for Caucasus and Central Asian oil and gas, a goal, it was suggested that Tehran shared with Moscow. Turkey was concerned too with Iran's support and aid to Armenia and its lukewarm relations with Azerbaijan in spite of the fact that Armenia still occupied 20 percent of that country as a result of the early 1990s war. Tehran, of course, was still miffed over its exclusion from various consortiums to lift and carry westward the oil from Azerbaijan's Caspian Sea basin wells. Tehran believed that Ankara acquiesced much too easily to the pressure of the U.S. to exclude Iran.

But there were other and more immediate concerns regarding the Kurds in the Ankara-Tehran axis. The most important was Turkey's belief that Iran provided succor to the PKK and supported it logistically, especially PKK camps along the Turkish-Iranian border. Iran, too, it was declared, provided medical services to the PKK—even to the guerrillas wounded in skirmishes in Turkey. Ankara alleged that Tehran had aided the PKK in northern Iraq as an instrument to expand its own influence in the region. Furthermore, in August 1996, Ankara still insisted that Iran supported an "understanding" between the PKK and the KDP and that it did so in cooperation with Syria. PKK-KDP cooperation would provide a potential corridor via northern Iraq between Syria and Iran. In short, Iran's increasing activities in northern Iraq since mid 1995 had made it a major player in northern Iraq. This was a role that Ankara did not like.

Ankara also thought that the growing presence of Iran in northern Iraq made it easier for the PKK to receive weapons from the Russian and Central Asian arms bazaars. PKK members also had the means to travel from Europe directly to northern Iraq via Iran. Ankara believed that the expanding presence of Iran in northern Iraq had substantially changed the balance of space that had existed in the region since the Persian Gulf war—a balance that up to 1995 had very much favored Turkey.

Erbakan's intention in Tehran to seek a solution to the PKK challenge was emphasized by the concurrent mission of Şevkat Kazan, minister of justice and Mehmet Sağlam, minister of education, both of whom were/are close confidants of Mr. Erbakan, and a coterie of other high profile businessmen in Baghdad. With the reopening of the Kirkuk-Yumurtalık oil pipelines that Ankara expected soon and which did occur later in the year (10 December) and the revenues resulting from the reopening, it was clear that one of the focuses of the Kazan-Sağlam talks with Baghdad was to discuss policies and establish measures to defeat the Kurdish challenge in all three countries.

The seriousness of the WP's efforts was reaffirmed by reports that Shaykh `Uthman, the leader of the Islamic Movement of Kurdistan (IMK), who controls a portion of northern Iraq centered on Ranya and adjacent to the Iranian border, was in Ankara on 11-12 August ostensibly to attend the wedding of his friend, İhsan Aslan, the director of a welfare organization in Ankara with close ties to the Naqsbaniyya Muslim order (*tarikat*) to which both Erbakan and Shaykh `Uthman were/are respected adherents. Notably Shaykh `Uthman made his journey to Ankara while Erbakan was in Tehran.

A third prong of the 11-12 August diplomatic offensive were reports that Hafiz al-Asad had invited Erbakan to Damascus to discuss outstanding issues between the two countries. From Tehran, Erbakan announced that a summit among the "big four" would take place in Damascus in September, a report that the Turkish foreign ministry labeled as unfounded. The TAF was strongly opposed to such a meeting and it did not take place.

There were domestic political reasons for Erbakan's intense desire to bring the PKK to heel. Eleven Kurdish MPs of the WP declared in a July meeting with the prime minister that if some Kurdish demands—education in Kurdish, job creation, a Kurdish TV channel (interestingly, a channel to be setup in northern Iraq in order to circumvent Turkish constitutional restrictions), a fair court system, etc.—were not implemented, that they and also some 25 to 45 MPs from the southeastern provinces, would possibly leave the WP. The abdication of even 33 MPs from the WP would have meant a 25 percent reduction of total parliamentary members of the WP. Such an abandonment would have spelled the end of the WP as a viable political party, let alone a contending one. Tehran was no doubt well apprised and took into consideration Erbakan's precarious domestic position and the importance of his Kurdish constituency during the August talks. From Erbakan's visit to Tehran in early August 1996 to February 1997 relations between the two neighbors improved, but suspicions regarding each other's intentions in northern Iraq and Turkey's continued charges that Iran was giving sanctuary to the PKK remained major irritants. The 31 August 1996 attack by the KDP in alliance with Baghdad against Tehran's PUK ally, which caught Iran by surprise, caused the next eruption between the two countries.

The late August alliance between Ankara, the KDP and Baghdad to oust Iran's PUK ally from Arbil and the surrounding hinterland, through which potential oil or gas pipelines might cross caused major differences. The KDP alliance with Baghdad and the swiftness of their initial victories surprised Tehran. Iran was about to experience a reduction of influence in the region that it had so assiduously built up after the Drogeda agreements. The reasons for the KDP alliance with Baghdad were several: 1) the KDP felt threatened by the increasingly close ties of the PUK with Iran; 2) Barzani was upset that Talabani had facilitated an Iranian incursion of some 3,000 to 4,000 troops through some 50 miles of PUK-held territory in late July ostensibly for attacking an IKDP base in KDP-controlled territory just north of the 36th parallel; and 3) the KDP leader no doubt thought that the PUK-facilitated Iranian incursion manned by Iraqi Shi'i troops heralded further assaults into his territory by the PUK supported by Iran. More Iranian-supported PUK attacks on the KDP's southern boundaries would have compelled the KDP to deploy more of its *peshmergas* in the south, limiting its ability to attack the PKK in northern Iraq in cooperation with the TAF.[76] Even prior to the incursion, the KDP realized that Turkey was ready to extend its international border 9 to 15 miles into KDP-controlled territories in order to staunch PKK attacks. This was anticipated to be an area in which the Turks would try to limit the KDP to only a token presence.

Prior to 31 August 1996, Barzani realized the possibility of the reduction of both his northern and southern controlled areas. Barzani also, no doubt, thought that any opening of the Kirkuk-Yumurtalık pipelines and the revenues resulting from it would weaken his position vis à vis the PUK. The KDP leader thought, correctly it seems, that neither the U.S. nor its European allies via Operation Provide Comfort (OPC) and the host of NGOs that they directly or indirectly controlled would seek to strengthen his position to the level that he thought appropriate. Barzani realized that the reopening of the oil pipeline and Baghdad's increased trade with Turkey would mean that he no longer would be able to control exclusively the then estimated $250,000 to $300,000 per day truck trade crossing the Turkish-Iraqi border at Habur/Khabur.[77]

In early 1996, the Turks had also approved the establishment of a Kurdish Conservative Party. A small marginal group in northern Iraq that advocated the creation of an independent state of Mosul, to include Kurds and Arabs, that would cooperate with Turkey and act as a buffer against a truncated Iraq. Throughout 1996 and 1997, Ankara also strengthened its

---

[76]Robert Olson, "Why the KDP?" *Kurdistan Report*, no. 24, November-December 1996, 23.

[77]*Ibid.*

ties with the Iraqi Turkmen and with the Iraq National Turkmen Party headquartered in Ankara. Turkmen comprise a community of some 500,000 people in northern Iraq and look to Turkey for support. Tehran joined the PKK in condeming the closer ties between Ankara and the Turkmen. Although Ankara intended its relationship with the Turkmen to be a hedge against Kurdish separatist aspirations, Tehran did not like the close association between Ankara, the KDP and the Turkmen.[78]

Tehran was probably surprised by the alacrity with which the KDP and Baghdad agreed upon and implemented their alliance. Tehran no doubt realized, however, that Baghdad's biggest need was to open the roads and the pipelines from Baghdad to the Turkish border in order to increase its trade with Turkey and to loosen the noose of the UN economic sanctions. Baghdad needed the KDP to achieve this objective. The alliance also allowed Saddam Husayn's government to get rid of several thousand Kurds who collaborated with the U.S., OPC and Western NGOs, thereby reducing attacks and plots against him and his government launched from that region.

Iran reacted slowly to the Baghdad-KDP-Ankara alliance. President Rafsanjani was visiting African countries and Tehran was able to do little to help the PUK forces as they fled the KDP-Baghdad assault. Many PUK *peshmerga* fled to Iran itself. However, by the end of 1996, the PUK with support from Tehran, had managed to recover most of the territory it had lost to the KDP in September. The 31 August battle and subsequent war between the two Kurdish groups seemed to sound the death knell of any potentially strong and united Kurdish autonomous entity in northern Iraq. Fighting between the two groups continued throughout 1997.

In late 1996 there were attempts by Turkey to bring the two warring Kurdish factions to some kind of agreement. The so-called "Ankara process" began at the end of October 1996. It consisted of renewed mediation efforts by the U.S., Turkey and Britain to end the KDP-PUK war. The Ankara process continued into the spring of 1997. But it came to an end with the massive Turkish incursion into northern Iraq in May. One of the reasons for the failure of the Ankara process was Iranian opposition. The very name of the negotiations "Ankara process" was enough to turn the Iranians off. The Iranians excoriated U.S. policies

---

[78]Phebe Marr, "Turkey and Iraq," in Henri J. Barkey, ed. *Reluctant Neighbor: Turkey's Role in the Middle East* (Washington, D.C.: United States Institute of Peace Press, 1996), 61.

stating that the aim of the negotiations was to create "a spying base and spring board to carry out malicious schemes in the region."[79] Tehran continued to repeat its consistent mantra that the U.S. intended to create another Israel in northern Iraq.

The August-September 1996 KDP-PUK war did, however, help restore equilibrium in Tehran's and Ankara's relationship. The KDP-PUK war allowed both capitals to reinforce their influence with each of their proxies. This in turn allowed both countries to better manage their respective geopolitical concerns regarding the Kurdish question in northern Iraq. But this refurbished equilibrium soon crumbled in February 1997 due to the Sinjan affair.

The Sinjan Affair and Its Impact

Sinjan is a small town of 3,000 people about 40 kilometers from Ankara. On the weekend of 31 January-2 February 1997 the town staged a "Jerusalem Memorial Night." The memorial was initiated by Ayatollah Khomeini and had been held in Iran for the past 17 years on the last Friday of Ramadan. It also occurred on the anniversary of the Islamic revolution in Iran. Sinjan is a conservative town that firmly supported the WP, as did its mayor, Bekir Yıldız. The organizers of the Jerusalem night memorial planned a gala occasion for which they had put up posters of Abbas Musavi, Musa Sadr and Fathi Shakaki, Hizbollah and Hamas leaders in Lebanon and among the Palestinians. The municipal leaders of Sinjan invited the Iranian Ambassador to Turkey Mohammad Reza Baqeri and PLO representative in Turkey Mahmud bin Yassini to speak.

Baqeri reportedly criticized Israel stating, "The English gave birth to this illegitimate child and the Americans raised it. They [the Americans] are still helping it to grow and providing it with force. In its [Israel's] war with the Arabs, if America had not protected it, this illegitimate child would not have lived."[80] Baqeri reportedly told the approximately 500 some people who attended the memorial not to be afraid to be called radical; he implored the crowd to follow the *shari'a*. The event of Sinjan created a political fire storm in Turkey, marking the beginning of the end

---

[79]Hasan Alsalih, " U.S. Intervention Will Only Aggravate Conflict," *Kayhan International*, 13 March 1997.

[80]I have taken this account of the Sinjan affair from the *Hürriyet, Cumhuriyet* and *TRKNWS-L* internet news service.

of the Erbakan government. Oppositional parties and the TAF said the events that took place in Sinjan were an attack on secularism and the basis of the modern republic of Turkey. The TAF found the developments in Sinjan intolerable. On 4 February they sent some 50 tanks, armored personnel carriers and other military vehicles through Sinjan's main street called, ironically and symbolically, Atatürk boulevard. The TAF claimed that the tanks were on their way to military maneuvers at a nearby army camp. But everyone got the message. Bekir Yıldız, the mayor of Sinjan, was indicted, and the State Security Court demanded he receive a 19.5-year prison sentence, and his 11 accomplices, almost all of whom were bureaucrats in the Sinjan municipality, 10-year prison terms.

The Iranians proclaimed that they had done or said nothing in Sinjan that they had not said before in Turkey for the past 17 years upon being invited to such gatherings. The Erbakan government tried to prevent or at least postpone the expulsion of Baqeri and other Iranians from Turkey which oppositional leaders and the TAF were demanding. Mesut Yılmaz, the leader of the Motherland Party (MP), who was appointed prime minister after Erbakan's ouster, said that Baqeri "is not a diplomat; he is a terrorist." He demanded that Baqeri and Mohammad Reza Rashid, Iranian head consul in İstanbul, be sent home immediately. Yılmaz and the TAF prevailed, and on 19 February Baqeri and Rashid were declared *persona non grata* and expelled. Tehran said the two diplomats would return to Turkey after a brief stay in Iran, but the two never returned.

In addition to Baqeri and Rashid, Said Zare, the Iranian consul in Erzurum, was also expelled on 1 March for remarks critical of General Çevik Bir's statements while in Washington, D.C., in early February, when he attended the American-Turkish Business Council annual meeting and at which he declared Iran to be a "state that supported terrorism." Zare also criticized the TAF for sending tanks to Sinjan: "Are tanks not an expression of violence? How can this be in compliance with the principle of a state of law?"[81] Immediately after Bir's remarks, Iran's foreign ministry summoned Turkey's ambassador and told him that Bir's remarks in Washington were "ugly" and that they were unfitting for any Turkish official to make. Iran retaliated for the expulsion of its diplomats by evicting Osman Korutürk, Turkey's ambassador to Iran and Ufuk Özsancak, Turkish consul in Urmiya. Önur Öymen, undersecretary of the foreign ministry, speaking at the Washington Institute for Near East

---

[81]*Iran Times*, 7 March 1997.

Studies, a pro-Israeli think tank, after Ankara's decision to expel the two Iranian diplomats, stated, "Although it is necessary to use diplomatic language in our relations with Iran, so far it has proved unsatisfactory. Their support of terrorism cannot be part of good neighborly relations." He said, "We can choose our friends, but we cannot choose our neighbors." Öymen emphasized that "half" of Iran's population speaks Turkish and has "strong cultural and ethnic links to Turkey." He added, however, that Turkey's dependence on oil imports made good relations with Iran essential."[82]

---

[82]*TRKNWS-L*, 21 February 1997.

CHAPTER SIX

The Israelis, the Islamists and the Mykonos Verdict

The Israeli-Turkish Alliance and Its Impact on Turkish-Iranian Relations

The Sinjan affair had barely subsided when Ankara-Tehran relations cooled further. The cause of the cooling was the 24-28 February visit of Chief of the General Staff Ismail Hakkı Karadayı to Israel. It was the first visit of a Turkish Chief of the General Staff to the Jewish state. Karadayı's visit occurred amidst a blitz of military, educational, economic and trade agreements between Ankara and Tel Aviv. The Turkey-Israel alliance raised speculation about a new axis of power in the Middle East that, with the backing of the U.S. and Europe, was intended to dominate the Middle East and Eastern Mediterranean.[83]

Before leaving for Israel, Karadayı stressed that one of the issues he would discuss with his Israeli counterparts, in addition to the procedures for implementing the agreements already signed, was the transfer of short-range Russian made Scud missiles from Iran to Syria. The Chief of the General Staff claimed that the missiles were flown to Syria from Iran over Turkish airspace in cargo aircraft. Although the Iranians labeled the cargo "humanitarian aid," Karadayı stressed that such missiles deployed on the Syrian border with Israel would be able to reach Israeli settlements and towns. He said further that he would emphasize to his Israeli colleagues that Turkey was also apprehensive that the missiles could fall into the hands of the PKK, who might use them for attacks against and within Turkey. Karadayı stopped his interview at this point, leaving everyone to speculate what Israel could do to stop the Iranian transfer of

---

[83]For these developments see Robert Olson, "Israel and Turkey: Consolidating Relations," *Middle East International*, no. 547, 4 April 1997, 16-7.

missiles that Turkey itself seemed unwilling to prevent.[84]

The frequent diplomatic and military traffic between Ankara and Tel Aviv in the spring of 1997 worried Tehran. On 8-10 April Israel's Foreign Minister David Levy visited Turkey and Turkish Defense Minister Turhan Tayan was in Tel Aviv during 30 April-2 May. Tayan's visit was followed by that of General Çevik Bir on 4-5 May. Levy met with Karadayı and Foreign Minister Çiller both of whom emphasized that Syria and Iran were "headquarters of terrorism" that threatened Turkey and Israel. During his stay in Israel, Tayan used every opportunity in his meetings with President Weizman and Prime Minister Netanyahu to stress that the Israel-Turkey pacts were directed against the "terrorist supporting countries of Iran and Syria." He also accused Iran and Syria of making and stockpiling ballistic missiles.

Tayan mentioned repeatedly that the main objective of the Turkish-Israeli alliance was to fight "terrorism." He charged that the "terrorism" threatening Israel and Turkey was headquartered in Damascus and that Iran supported, supplied and protected the PKK and Hamas. The defense minister stated that Ankara and Tel Aviv were in constant contact and exchanged intelligence information regarding their mutual "terrorism" threat. Tayan proclaimed that support of "terrorism" by Iran, Iraq and Syria was a threat not only to Turkey and Israel but also to the entire region and to NATO countries as well. Via Israel the Turkish defense minister tried to further internationalize the Kurdish question. Concerning the situation in northern Iraq, Tayan said that "Turkey would not stand still and allow the "security-less" north of Iraq become "a swamp of terrorism."[85]

On 5 May the Iranian media, reflecting government opinion, responded that Tayan's comments while in Israel did not promote good neighborly relations: "In the long run," said the *Tehran Times*, "Turkey may experience what has happened in Algeria." Tehran was particularly upset by Tayan's charges that Iran and Syria were manufacturing chemical weapons and ballistic missiles. "In spite of Prime Minister Erbakan's efforts to follow an independent policy some Turkish generals are trying to deliver their country to Washington and Tel Aviv," continued the *Times*.[86]

---

[84]*Ibid.* 11; *Hürriyet*, 24 February 1997.

[85]*Hürriyet*, 5 May 1997; *TRKNWS-L*, 2, 3, 4 May 1997.

[86]*Tehran Times*, 4 May 1997.

The concern of Iran and Syria throughout 1997 was to foster an alliance, *de facto* or *in situ*, of other countries to counter the Ankara-Tel Aviv alliance. There were frequent high level visits and talks between Tehran and Damascus. In late July President Hafiz al-Asad of Syria visited Iran to pay his respects to outgoing President Rafsanjani and to talk with new President Mohammad Khatami. Asad was accompanied by a coterie of generals to discuss "strategic regional cooperation"—how to counter the Israel-Turkey alliance.[87]

The full implications of the Turkey-Israel alliance cannot be discussed here, but some of its implications are clear: 1) Ankara wants Israel's and the American Jewish community's support for their efforts to crush the PKK and to suppress Kurdish nationalism; 2) Turkey hopes that closer relations with Israel and U.S. Jews will dampen any further American Jewish criticism of their ethnic cleansing of Kurds in southeast Turkey; 3) Ankara seeks Jewish support to put pressure on Syria to no longer harbor or support the PKK in Syria or elsewhere; 4) the TAF hopes to demonstrate its continued orientation toward the West in spite of its diminished geostrategic importance in the wake of the collapse of the Soviet Union; 5) the Kemalist elite and the TAF hope to demonstrate their commitment to secularism and to refuse to allow any Islamist-based party to come to power; 6) the promotion of closer relations with Israel by Ankara and the TAF while an Islamist government was in power demonstrated that an avowedly anti-Israeli government, in rhetoric at least, was unable to deter the consolidating relationship; 7) Turkey needs the technological might of Israel both for its military and industrial improvement; 8) both Ankara and Tel-Aviv are engaged in the ethnic cleansing of their largest minority populations and their alliance serves to suppress any criticism regarding each's ethnic cleansing from either country and hence from other sources; 9) both countries try to legitimatize their ethnic cleansing practices by emphasizing their needs for economic expansion in order to become even more valuable allies of the West; and 10) it seems that Tel Aviv hopes to gain more influence over the Euphrates waters by investing in the GAP project. By doing so, Israel, in conjunction with Turkey, hopes to use the "water card" against the Arabs' "oil card" in order to secure its anticipated energy needs. In return, Tel Aviv must help Ankara to crush the PKK and control its Kurdish

---

[87]Michael Jansen, "Asad on Tour," *Middle East International*, 8 August 1997.

challenge.[88]

Philip Robins suggests that Israel and Turkey are also drawn together by their sympathetic political cultures.   Both countries have institutionalized and routinized politics to a much further degree than the Arab states.   Few Arab states have functioning legislatures, fewer still have independent judiciaries.   Robins argues that the institionalization of politics in Turkey and Israel makes for policy continuity.   The lack of policy continuity and personalization of politics in Arab countries makes the Kemalist elite of Turkey uncomfortable.[89]

The implications for Turkey and Syrian relations are clear.   One of the purposes of the alliance is to compel Syria to accept the dictates of the U.S. and Israel in the "peace process" negotiations.   Ankara hopes to use the leverage of Tel Aviv on Washington to make Damascus expel Abdullah Öcalan and other PKK operatives.   Such an expulsion would weaken Syria's ability to use the PKK as an instrument against Turkey in its demands for an equal share of the Euphrates river waters. It would wreak havoc with Syria's ability to be a major player in the politics of northern Iraq and it would lessen Syria's usefulness to Iran as an ally in the eastern Mediterranean.   It would also result in a reduction of the instruments that Tehran and Damascus have to encourage Ankara to be more amenable to the concerns of the two countries in terms of water, trade, regional and wider geostrategic alliances. The PKK is a necessary and an extremely useful card for Tehran and Damascus to play against

---

[88]For some analysis of the alliance see Robert Olson, "Turkey-Syria Relations," 178-91. For one of the fullest treatments of Israel-Turkey relations see, Alan Makovsky, "Israeli-Turkish Relations: A Turkish "Periphery Strategy"? in Henri J. Barkey, *Reluctant Neighbor: Turkey's Role in the Middle East* (Washington, D.C.: United States Institute of Peace Press, 1996), 147-70; Robert Olson, "The Turkey-Israel Agreement and the Kurdish Question," *Middle East International*, no. 526, 24 May 1996, 18-19; Robert Olson, "An Israeli-Kurdish Conflict?" *Middle East International*, no. 529, 5 July 1996, 17; Robert Olson, "Israel and Turkey-Consolidating Relations," *Middle East Intrnational*, no. 547, 4 April 1997, 16-17; Robert Olson, "Israel and the Kurds: PKK the Target," *Middle East International*, no. 544, 21 February 1997, 14; Robert Olson, "Turkey, Israel and American Jews," *Middle East International*, 559, 26 September 1997, 16-17.

[89]Philip Robins, "Avoiding the Question," in Henri J. Barkey, ed. *Reluctant Neighbor: Turkey's Role in the Middle East* (Washington, D.C.: United States Institute of Peace Press, 1996), 181-2.

Ankara, not only because of the challenge and expense of Ankara's war against the PKK in Turkey and in northern Iraq but also to the continued growth of the Kurdish problem in Turkey as the paramount problem confronting the state as it is presently structured. The challenge of trying to accommodate, control, feed and employ the 3 million Kurdish refugees in western Turkey is monumental enough in itself.[90]

Although Iran and Syria wish to use the PKK and the Kurdish card against Turkey, they do not want Ankara to become so provoked that it will go to war or attack the PKK bases in either country as it has done in northern Iraq since 1983. Both Tehran and Damascus want a managed "Kurdish question." But its management has become increasingly difficult with the new alliances between Turkey and Israel. Iran and Syria are able to pursue this strategy because they both think that their own Kurdish problems are more manageable than are Turkey's, and they are correct in this assessment. But the Turks' alliance with the Israelis may embolden Ankara to take stronger actions than it has in the past against Tehran and Damascus. This in turn jeopardizes the manner in which the two countries would like to play their Kurdish cards.

The creation of a Kurdish state in northern Iraq, although after 1994 a clearly unlikely development, would affect much more strongly the Kurds in Turkey than in Iran or Syria. As I argued above, none of the three countries want an independent Kurdish state. As far as Iran and Syria are concerned, it would be a second Israel in their midst. The trans-state aspects of the Kurdish question must make Ankara wish that all of the Kurds in the Middle East resided in Turkey, reducing their usefulness as instruments against Turkey. But Tehran's and Syria's policies have always faced a danger, i.e., that Turkey would seek an alliance with Israel to help contain the Kurdish question and thereby provide time for Ankara to deal more effectively and coercively with its Kurdish problem. This is exactly what Ankara did in 1996 in a pronounced fashion, although the two countries had close relations on a number of issues for some years. If one of the reasons for Turkey to ally strongly with Israel was to receive support to help it contain or to eliminate completely the PKK whose war

---

[90]The encompassing parameters of the Kurdish problem in Turkey are addressed in a recent scholarly study (although from a nationalist Turkish perspective) by Kemal Kirişci and Gareth M. Winrow, *The Kurdish Question in Turkey: An Example of a Trans-State Ethnic Conflict* (London: Frank Cass, 1997). The Turkish translation is entitled *Kürt Sorunu: Kökeni ve Gelişimi* (İstanbul: Tarih Vakfı Yurt Yayınları, no. 47, 1997).

against Ankara Tehran and Damascus were supporting, than Syria and Iran got more than they bargained for. Their policies of using the Kurds against Turkey resulted in a deep and broad alliance that threatens both Iran's and Syria's wider geopolitical and geostrategical concerns, which are not just influenced by the trans-state Kurdish question or the intrastate Kurdish problem. It is important to remember in this new line-up that Israel does not have a Kurdish problem nor is it affected in any direct way by the trans-state Kurdish question. But it is in a position to pursue policies that influence either or both issues. This is a good example of a bi-lateral, or when Syria is included, a tri-lateral trans-state ethnic problem that has assumed wider regional dimensions and, by virtue of that fact plays a role in international affairs: the latter because it directly affects the Israel-Palestinian "peace process." It is this dimension that obviously impelled President Asad's late July 1997 visit to Tehran.

Despite the mutual diplomatic expulsions of late February and early March, President Demirel sent Turkish Foreign Ministry Undersecretary Ali Tugan as a special envoy to convey his and the Turkish peoples' condolences for the devastating earthquake that struck Ardabil on 28 February. Tugan met with Deputy Foreign Minister for Asia-Pacific Affairs Allaadin Boroujerdi who thanked Tugan and said that the dispatch of a special envoy showed the importance Turkey attached to its ties with Iran, adding that "Iran has been following the same policy towards its relations with Ankara." Earlier in the same day, Secretary of the Supreme National Security Council Hassan Rouhaim stated, "The problems arising in Tehran-Ankara relations have been caused by U.S. engineered plots."[91]

Tugay's main message to Tehran was apparently not criticism of the recent diplomatic evictions, but to express Ankara's unhappiness with Tehran's continued support of the PKK. The special envoy stressed in private talks that in the Turkish view Iran was not carrying out the security agreements it had signed with Turkey regarding the two countries' border security. Tugan reportedly told Rafsanjani that "If Tehran did not cooperate with Turkey against the PKK and stop meddling in its internal affairs the two countries' relations would continue to worsen."[92]

---

[91]*Ettela'at*, 4 March 1997.

[92]*Hürriyet*, 3 March 1997.

The Kurdish Question, the Islamist Challenge and the Ouster of Erbakan

Turkey's and Iran's mutual expulsion of diplomats occurred largely because of Ankara's concern with the growth and increasing popularity of political Islam and the growth of "Islamic capital," i.e., the rise of a provincial Anatolian bourgeoisie trying to loosen the shackles of the national and international capitalists of the large cities in the west. The combination of political Islam and Islamic capital was an explosive mixture presenting a serious challenge to the TAF-backed western, international, capitalist elites. The Sinjan affair encouraged further the TAF to oust the Erbakan government, which they succeeded in doing four months later. The late February and March expulsion of diplomats was only the second such expulsion since the Iranian revolution in 1979. The first time, as mentioned earlier, was Ankara's expulsion of Iranian Ambassador to Turkey Manushehr Motaki in April 1989 for expressing his country's dissatisfaction with Turkey's lack of a "firm stand" against Salman Rushdie's *Satanic Verses*. Ankara was also unhappy with Motaki's and other Iranian diplomats' support for the right of Turkish women to wear the *hijab*, which in Turkey consisted of light-weight raincoats unlike the head to toe black *chador* worn by Iranian women. The Turkish press had reported that Ali Asghar Shafi`i, the Iranian consul in Erzurum, had distributed copies of Ayatollah Khomeini's death threat against Rushdie to the *müftüs* (religious judges) in eastern Anatolia for dissemination among the Kurdish and Alevi population.[93]

Turkish Grand National Assembly Speaker Yıldırım Akbulut had chastised the Iranian *majlis* for reading a letter signed by 150 deputies condemning the ban on the *hijab*. The sensitivity of the *hijab* issue in Turkish politics was emphasized when the ban on *hijabs* was lifted on 28 December 1989. The *Satanic Verses*, however, continued to play a strong role in Turkish-Iranian relations. On 2 July 1993, Islamist rioters set afire a hotel in Sıvas, a city of several hundred thousand in east-central Turkey on the fault line between Sunni-Alevi populations, which has a large Kurdish and Turkish population. Sıvas was hosting a convention of leftist intellectuals and writers, many of whom were Alevi and Kurdish. Islamists, supposedly largely from the city of Sıvas and comprised of Sunnis, accused the conventioneers of spreading atheism. One of the

---

[93]*The Middle East Journal*, "Chronology," vol. 43, no. 3 (1989):504.

primary targets of the Islamists was Aziz Nesin, who had recently, as mentioned earlier, published excerpts of the *Satanic Verses*. Nesin managed to escaped unharmed from the hotel in which 40 people died.

The tension over the Sinjan affair, Çevik Bir's statements that Iran was a state that supported terrorism and the Turkey-Israel treaties of 1996 kept tension high between the two states throughout 1997. Four days after Ambassador Korutürk returned to Turkey on 6 March, Iranian Foreign Minister Akbar Veliyati was in Ankara to invite President Demirel to the Organization of the Islamic Conference (OIC) to be held in Tehran in December. Demirel said he would attend the OIC meeting and "would make every effort to have a successful meeting of the OIC in Tehran," a gesture that would give an added boost to new President Mohammad Khatami. The Turkish President repeated again that "relations between Turkey and Iran had been good ever since the Treaty of Kasr-i Shirin in 1639." Veliyati stressed in his response "the need for good relations between the two countries and that both governments had taken measures to bolster and rebuild their mutual relations."[94] Turkish Minister of Energy and Natural Resources Recai Kutan stressed the need for good relations. He said diplomatic relations continued at the chargé d'affaires level and, furthermore, mutual economic activities were continuing despite the cooling in diplomatic relations. Kutan noted that Turkey would need 27 billion cubic meters of gas annually by the year 2,000 and that Iran would be one of the major suppliers of gas to Turkey.[95] In 1997 Turkey imported 8 billion cubic meters of gas from Iran.

The 1989 and 1997 expulsion of ambassadors are the only two instances of a break in Turkey-Iran relations since the Islamic revolution in 1979. Both expulsions occurred as a result of Turkey's sensitivity to the role that Iranian officials played in encouraging the Islamist movement in Turkey. This certainly was the case in 1989. In the 1997 episode, it is clear that Iranian officials gave encouragement to Islamist currents. Although Turkey's concern regarding Iran's support of the PKK played a role in both expulsions, by 1997 the TAF was concerned by the cooperation and even the mutual interests of the Islamist movements and the PKK. PKK leader Öcalan frequently stated his approval of aspects of

---

[94]*Ettela'at*, 12 March 1997.

[95]*Ibid*, 17 March 1997.

the Islamist movement and of the policies of the WP, if not Erbakan himself, whom he considered a Kemalist "wrapped" in Islamist discourse. On 28 April in one of a series of "briefings," a euphemism for the public denounciations by the TAF and NSC of the Erbakan government, given throughout April and May, the NSC announced that the greatest threat facing the nation was not the PKK itself but the cooperation between the PKK and the Islamists, who were constantly called "reactionaries" (irticacılar). Less than six weeks later the TAF toppled Erbakan.

The Mykonos Verdict

The Mykonos verdict on 10 April 1997 by a German court did not disturb Iran-Turkey relations. Mykonos refers to a restaurant in Berlin where four assailants assassinated Sadegh Sharafkandi, the 54-year-old leader and Secretary-General of the KDPI; Fattah Abdouli, the party's European representative; and Homayum Ardalan, the party's German representative. Four other Iranian oppositional leaders were also killed. One of the assassins, Kazem Darabi, was described as an employee of the Iranian Intelligence Ministry who, according to the German court, had organized the assassination on orders, charged the German court, of Supreme Guide Ali Khamenehi and President Rafsanjani.[96] The Mykonos verdict completely disrupted diplomatic ties between Iran and the European Union (EU). The EU countries immediately recalled their ambassadors to Tehran, and Iran retaliated by recalling its diplomatic personnel from EU countries. The Mykonos verdict spelled the end of the "critical dialogue" that the EU had established with Iran in contrast to the "dual containment" policy of the U.S. Bitter recriminations flew between Bonn and Tehran throughout 1997. Even Mohammad Khatami's assumption of the presidency of Iran on 4 August did not ease the strain. German Foreign Minister Klaus Klinkel said that Khatami's proclaimed moderate polices offered only "a feeble glimmer of hope."[97]

The glimmer shortly turned incandescent. On 16 November 1997, 11 EU ambassadors returned to their posts in Tehran. The German ambasador, as demanded by Iranian protocol because of Tehran's belief

---

[96]Saeed Barzin, "Bitter Fruit of Mykonos," *Middle East International*, no. 548, 18 April 1997, 16.

[97]*Iran Times*, 8 August 1997.

that Bonn had acquiesced too easily to the Mykonos verdict, returned on 25 November. He was accompanied by the French ambassador as an EU face-saving measure. Switzerland which is not a member of the EU also returned its ambassador who had been withdrawn in sympathy with his EU colleagues. Thus by the end of November 1997 all EU ambasadors had returned to their posts in Tehran. The one exception was Great Britian which has not been represented at the ambassadorial rank in Tehran since 1989 when he was withdrawn as a result of British displeasure of the death *fetva* imposed on Salman Rushdie in 1989. London is represented by a charge d' affaires.

For all of the dispruption that the Mykonos affair and verdict caused to EU, U.S. and Iranian relations, it did not cause a ripple in Turkish-Iranian relations. The two capitals acted as if the tensions of February and March were forgotten. The Turkish foreign ministry said that it would "need time" to study the verdict and its implications. Ömer Akbel, the foreign ministry spokesman, said that "Turkish-Iranian relations are different from Turkey's relations with Germany and other EU countries because they are more direct and closer."[98]   Turkey did, of course, use the Mykonos verdict to proclaim its comprehensive disgust with and war against "terrorism."

[98]*Hürriyet*, 15 April 1997.

CHAPTER SEVEN

The Kurdish Question in 1997

The Turkish Incursions into Northern Iraq:The PKK Again

By May 1997 it was not the consequences of the Mykonos verdict but the PKK that again was on the front burner in Turkey-Iran relations. On 13 May, Turkey again struck into northern Iraq to attack PKK bases. The May attack was much larger than the incursions of 1992 and 1995. Turkish forces comprising of 50,000 to 60,000 troops backed by 200 to 300 tanks and several hundred armored carriers assisted by 10,000 KDP *peshmerga*, penetrated some 100 to 125 miles into Iraq. By the end of July when the bulk of its forces had been withdrawn, although several thousand still remained, Ankara proclaimed that it and its KDP ally had killed and captured over 3,000 PKK and destroyed all of its warehouses and storage places, including caves.

The scale and depth of the Turkish incursion concerned Tehran and raised questions that had been asked during the earlier campaigns, namely, whether Turkey would become too strong a presence in northern Iraq and in Iraq itself enabling it to influence the politics of the Persian Gulf. The last thing Tehran wanted was for another non-Gulf country to become a direct participant in its politics. Tehran was concerned that the KDP had become completely under the control of and dependent on Turkey. As a result Turkey would be in a position to control and influence the distribution of the oil resources in or through northern Iraq. Tehran reiterated its concern about having a large Turkish army so close to its border with Iraq and abutting its own Kurdish and Azeri populations. Concerned about good relations with Iran, Prime Minister Erbakan sought during the May-June period of the incursion constant reassurance from the TAF and General Karadayı that Turkish forces would not advance close to the Iranian border. He discouraged those commanders who wanted to pursue the fleeing PKK into Iran, which, in the end, Turkey did not do. Erbakan was able to deflect some of the flack that fell his way from

Tehran when General Karadayı announced that he had not even told the prime minister about the planned incursion for fear that he or other members of his government would leak the news to the PKK.

During its incursion Turkey pounded the PKK relentlessly, although it is unknown how effectively. The TAF complained constantly that Iran not only was giving sanctuary to the fleeing PKK but also was providing them with medical treatment and weapons. Tehran responded that no country in the region should violate the borders of its neighbors. On 29 May Turkey announced that it had killed 14 terrorists and captured one that had crossed the border from the village of Dambat in Iran. The TAF stated that the raid was just one of 15 PKK operations launched from Iran during the previous two weeks.[99] Ankara claimed that as of August 1997 50 terrorists had crossed the border at Dambat. During interrogation the captured terrorists confessed that Iran did nothing to stop their operations and that the Iranians provided them with help.

On 4 June the respective temperatures rose again when Ankara claimed that two of its helicopters were shot down by Russian-made SA-7B land to air missiles that the PKK may have received from Iran killing all 13 crew members on board. The shooting down of the helicopters became more of an issue when runmors surfaced that four ranking Israeli officers were aboard the helicopters.[100] Ankara singled out Iran as one of the countries supplying the PKK with such missiles. Other countries considered culpable were Russia, Serbia, Syria, Greece and the Greek Republic of Cyprus.[101] The downing of the helicopters and the accusation from Ankara that Iran seemed the most likely culprit dominated the relationship in June and July. Mesut Yılmaz, the leader of the Motherland Party and the successor to Erbakan after the latter's ouster on 18 June, said that if Iran were found to be providing the PKK with land to air missiles that it would be "a cause for war."[102]

The shooting down of the helicopters did not, however, affect the wider

---

[99]*TRKNWS-L*, 29 May 1997. Turkey said that three of the terrorists were Iranian, one a Syrian and one an Armenian.

[100]This was reportedly announced on the Arabic service of Radio Monte Carolo but I was unable to document the source.

[101]*Hürriyet*, 7 June, 1997.

[102]*TRKNWS-L*, 10 June 1997.

geopolitical concerns of the two countries. On 13-14 May, both Demirel and Rafsanjani attended meetings of the Economic Cooperation Organization (ECO) in Askhabad, Turkmenistan.[103] The Turkish incursion against the PKK in northern Iraq was not high on their agenda. Instead the two leaders concerned themselves with Iran's worries about the Turkey-Israel alliance and Iran's attempts to foster a counter alliance of Iran, Syria and Egypt. Demirel again warned Iran to stop encouraging the spread of the *shari'a* in Turkey.[104]

Demirel's representations to Rafsanjani in Askhabad were strong enough that on 9-10 June Iranian Deputy Foreign Minister Alaadin Boroujerdi flew to Ankara to allay Turkish concerns by explaining Tehran's support of the PKK was not what Ankara claimed. During Boroujerdi's visit the Turkish foreign ministry revealed that there had already been 49 meetings in 1997 between high level Turkish and Iranian officials to ascertain how to combat terrorism. Önur Öymen, foreign ministry undersecretary, said that he had spent five hours with Boroujerdi going page by page through an extensive file on terrorist activities emanating from Iran.[105] While Boroujerid was in Ankara, the governors of Van province in eastern Turkey and Khoy district in Iran met for their 14th border security sub-commission meeting. This commission was created so that both countries would inform the other of PKK activities in their respective regions. Despite their differences regarding the PKK, Boroujerdi informed the Turks that President Rafsanjani would be in Istanbul to attend the 15-16 June D-8 Meeting.

Throughout late May and until he was ousted on 18 June, the TAF and the Turkish media tried to depict Prime Minister Erbakan as not being critical enough of Iran and of almost being a traitor to the glorious cause of the TAF in its war against the PKK. In retrospect, this was part of the TAF's campaign to gain public support in their efforts to topple the WP.

Mesut Yılmaz was most critical of Erbakan. Obviously, Yılmaz probably knew by May that he would be selected to form a new government after the ouster of Erbakan. He charged that Erbakan's government had not done enough to pressure Iran, Syria and Armenia to

---

[103]The ECO is comprised of ten countries--the five Central Asian republics and Turkey, Iran, Pakistan, Afghanistan, Azerbaijan.

[104]*Cumhuriyet*, 13 May, 1997.

[105]*TRKNWS-L*, 11 June 1997.

not provide missiles to the PKK. He blamed Erbakan's pipe dream of D-8 cooperation. Referring to the downing of the helicopters, Yılmaz said that in order not to offend Iran, Erbakan had caused the deaths of 13 martyrs. The future prime minister reiterated his charge that, if it were true that Iran was supplying missiles to the PKK, then "Iran is the number one enemy of Turkey." Referring to the D-8 meeting that was to be held in Istanbul on 15-16 June, Yılmaz said that Erbakan "would use the meeting to shower his Iranian brothers with praises. This is not a matter that should be forgiven: it is a stance that should bring the nation to rebellion."[106] Yılmaz got his wish as Erbakan was ousted by the TAF on 18 June, symbolically just two days after the D-8 meeting.

The Toppling of the Welfare Party

The Kurdish question and Turkey-Iran relations played an important role in the TAF and its civilian backers' toppling of the WP from power. From February 1997 to his ouster on 18 June, a constant barrage of charges, threats and warnings came from the TAF, various clandestine organizations that it controlled and oppositional leaders that Erbakan's Islamist government and his "D-8 pipe dream" allowed Iran to more assertively provide diplomatic, military and financial support to the PKK.

It was not Ankara-Tehran differences over their respective policies and concerns regarding their Kurdish policies in northern Iraq that most concerned them in 1997; it was Ankara's worry that Tehran's aid for the Islamist movements in Turkey would strengthen and embolden their challenge to the secularist, pro-West, international capitalist sector of Turkish society.

By 1997 Iran had some 1,200 diplomatic, political, business and cultural personnel in Turkey, and they had an heeding Turkish and Kurdish audience. There are also 1 million to 1.5 million Iranians living in Turkey, most of whom came after the revolution in 1979. There is no question the Islamist challenge to the Kemalist elite and their TAF protectors is a home grown challenge.[107] The TAF and media attacks on the Erbakan government provided a good indication of their concerns. The TAF's accusations against Iran for supporting the Islamist movement

---

[106]*Hürriyet*, 10 June 1997.

[107]For more on this subject see Hakan Yavus, "Turkey: The Establishment against Liberalization," *Middle East International*, no. 556, 8 August 1997, 18.

that was always characterized as "reactionary" (irticai) served the purpose of creating a foil for their own inability to stem the tide of an Islamist-oriented provincial bourgeoisie growing in strength and ever more daring in challenging the Kemalist state. In the WP, this provincial Islamist elite, led by their big-city, engineer-technocratic leaders had an official party that gave expression to their economic, social, cultural and religious values and aspirations.[108] The liberalization of the Turkish economy after 1983 strengthened further these new elites. In Iran, the Turkish provincial elites and their leaders had an example of how classes similar to their own played an important role in the economy and in politics. The Kemalist elite and their TAF protectors were of course concerned about the presence of the Kurds among the new provincial and Anatolia bourgeoisie and their representation in the Islamist movement and in the WP. As mentioned earlier, the WP has 40 to 45 MPs who are of Kurdish origin. This is undoubtedly one of the reasons that starting in February 1997 that the NSC announced in a series of "briefings" that the "greatest threat facing the nation is not the PKK itself, but the cooperation between the PKK and the "reactionaries," i.e., the WP and its constituency. The NSC announced that it had written a new National Military Strategic Concept in which it emphasized that "internal threats were much greater to the Turkish state than external threats." The TAF claimed that they had evidence that "separatists," i.e., the PKK, and "reactionaries" were exchanging intelligence information and perpetrating joint "actions against the state."[109]

The developments of 1997 and the coup against Erbakan showed that the TAF and the Kemalist elite were compelled to characterize their internal Kurdish problem as an external problem, i.e., that it was caused by Iran and Syria. This was the first time since the Sheikh Said rebellion in 1925 that the Kemalist elite were compelled to do so. Given the depth of the challenge of Kurdish nationalism to the present structure of the Turkish state and its Kemalist, international capitalist, pro-West

---

[108]For the role of engineers in particular in the Islamist movement in Turkey see Nilüfer Göle, "Secularism and Islamism in Turkey: The Making of Elites and Counter-Elites," *The Middle East Journal*, vol. 51, no. 1 (1997):46-57; and Göle, "Authoritarian Secularism and Islamist Politics: The Case of Turkey," in *Civil Society in the Middle East*, ed. Augustus Richard Norton (New York: E. J. Brill, 1996):17-43.

[109]*Hürriyet*, 29 April 1997.

configuration, the WP was perceived as a danger to their power. It seems that, at first, the Kemalist elite and the TAF were willing to allow the WP an opportunity to coopt the more militant Kurdish nationalist groups such as the PKK in order to reduce the attractiveness of the PKK and to enlist moderate Kurdish nationalists to cooperate politically to eliminate the PKK. But the one-year tenure of Erbakan's WP indicated to them that this would be impossible and Erbakan was ousted.

In spite of the significant role that the trans-state Kurdish question and the intrastate Kurdish problems have played in Turkish and Iranian history and politics, they have generally acted as a sub-stratum concern that has not affected the larger geostrategic interests of either state, whether in the Ottoman, Safavid or Qajar periods or in the post-WW I national states. In the 1990s, the reiteration of leaders of Turkey and Iran that relations have been good between the two countries since the Treaty of Kasr-i Shirin in 1639, has merit. Boundaries have changed little since then with the exception in the Caucasus. This is also true of the boundary defined after WW I as the Iraq-Iran border. The major struggle of redefinition of borders between the two states' spheres of interest has been in Iraq. Throughout the 1990s, Süleyman Demirel, during the period that he was prime minister of Turkey (1991-1993) and president (1993-), and Bülent Ecevit, leader of the Democratic Socialist Party (DSP) who became deputy prime minister in the Yılmaz government after Erbakan's ouster, advocated that the border between Turkey and Iraq should be moved about 15 miles southward.[110] This included the areas that Turkey had *de facto* made into a security zone after its 1992 incursion. No such recommendation was ever made regarding the border with Iran. This is in spite of the fact that the existing international borders among all three countries were partially determined by the presence of the Kurds and, in the case of Iraq and Turkey, entirely so. Because of the Kurdish nationalist challenge that Turkey and Iran have faced through much of the twentieth century, and especially after WW I, both states and their leaders have recognized that this internal challenge and the manipulation of it by each country far outweighs whatever short term advantages that either could achieve by direct interference in each other's internal politics.

The concerns of the Ottoman, Safavid and Qajar empires changed, of course, over time and are different from those of the modern states. But

---

[110]This was advocated repeatedly by Ecevit and Demirel from 1992 throughout 1997.

the Treaty of 1639, with the exceptions of the modifications mentioned earlier, represented a solid understanding of the spheres of influence of both empires: an understanding that even withstood the challenge of Nadir Shah from 1730 to 1747. In explaining an historical situation reminiscent of the late twentieth century, Ernest Tucker suggests that there was a conceptual breakthrough in Ottoman-Iranian relations in 1736. Tucker argues that the conceptual change was based on the doctrine of *darura* (legal necessity) that "emphasized a policy of peace based on recognizing the common Muslim identity of the two sides was generally preferable to a policy of conflict based on their differences." The recognition would preserve "the ideal of a single *umma* while formally recognizing the autonomy and special circumstances of individual Muslim countries."[111] It is important to stress that the ideal of a single *umma* that helped to moderate policies between the two empires did not continue after the creation of national states in the post-WW I era. Up to 1979 in Iran and to the present in Turkey, the two countries' acceptance of their respective national identities solicited mutual respect for each other's boundaries. The situation changed with the revolution in Iran when it again reverted to an Islamic orientation, but with a strong Iranian nationalist and Shi'i orientation. The Islamic orientation was sufficient, at least for the first two decades, to accommodate the largely Sunni Kurdish population. The fact that one and a half million Kurds are Shi'i aided the new regime in containing Kurdish nationalism, especially after 1983. One could argue that the Islamic revolution actually helped to contain what could have been an even stronger Kurdish nationalist movement. The same can be said for aiding the regime in containing potential Azeri nationalism. The fact there are a number of Azeris among the high clergy in Iran and among the ranks of the 200 ayatollahs and the fact that after 1989, and it is probably not a coincidence, the *veliyat-e faqih* or Supreme Guide, Ali Khamenehi, is an Azeri, also helped.

This was not the case in Turkey. The struggle in Turkey in the 1980s and 1990s was how and by what circumstances the state was going to accommodate the challenge of Kurdish nationalism. From 1984 to the present, the state has adopted the strategy of war. During this time it has

---

[111]For more on Nadir Shah's challenge to the Treaty of Kasr-i Shirin see Robert Olson, *The Siege of Mosul and Ottoman-Persian Relations, 1718-1747* (Indiana University Press, 1975), 185-99; Ernest Tucker, "The Peace Negotiations of 1736: A Conceptual Turning Point in Ottoman-Persian Relations," *The Turkish Studies Bulletin*, vol. 20, no. 1 (1996):16-37.

made little progress in recognizing Kurdish nationalism or even Kurdish cultural rights in terms of language, broadcasting or publishing. The population of the Kurds in Turkey is around 20 percent, while in Iran it is less than 10 percent. About 15 percent of Kurds in Iran are Shi'i while in Turkey 10 to 15 percent are Alevi, a branch of Islam close to the twelver shi'ism predominant in Iran. But the religious mosaic in Turkey is complicated further by the fact that approximately 20 percent of Turks are also Alevi. This means that significant numbers of Kurds in Turkey, as well as Turkish Alevis, find attractive the Islamist discourse emanating from Iran. In addition, like the Kurds in Turkey, many Alevis also harbor disgruntlement and feel that they too have been discriminated against by the nationalist Kemalist discourse of Turkey that, no matter how secularist, still smacks of Sunnism to them. There is in Turkey a Shi'i affiliated challenge in addition to the predominantly Sunni-led Islamist challenge to the Kemalist elite and the PKK-led Kurdish nationalist challenge. However, during the last decade the Turkish government has taken steps to reduce Alevi grievances by recognizing their national holidays such as *Nevroz*, the Alevi and Shi'is' New Year, and allowing them to openly practice their religious and cultural rituals. There are, however, a large number of unhappy Kurdish and Turkish Alevis.

Even if Iran did nothing to meddle, interfere or encourage such groups in Turkey, which potentially it could do, it would be logical that any Kemalist government in Turkey would accuse it of doing so in order to externalize its own internal threats. Since the Kemalist elite exercise power through a legitimated, ethnically based, Turkish nationalist discourse, it is easy for them to accuse Iran of aiding and abetting the PKK. This is an example of how a state externalizes a challenging internal threat.

CHAPTER EIGHT

Summary

The Kurdish Question and Its Effects on Iran's Geopolitical and Geostrategical Concerns in the 1990s

The Kurdish question in its trans-state and intrastate dimensions has not significantly affected the larger geopolitical and geostrategical interests of either Iran or Turkey in the 1980s and 1990s.[112] Here I shall address only those aspects of Iran's foreign policy that affect or bear upon the Kurdish question and not its comprehensive policies. Iran's foreign policy interests with regard to the Kurdish question are influenced by several factors. Iran does not want the Kurdish question or its own Kurdish problem to affect or influence substantially the Azeri question or Turkey's ability to use the Azeri question, whether in Azerbaijan itself or among the Azeri population in Iran. As I have stressed above, Iran has tried to mitigate this possibility.

Tehran fears that closer ties between Turkey and Israel will also increase ties between Baku and Tel Aviv. Tehran thinks that the Turkey-Israel alliance will give Israel an entree into the Caucasus and especially to Azerbaijan. Iran's worst fears were realized when Prime Minister Netanyahu visited Baku on 29 August on his return from a trip to East Asia. It was reported that Netanyahu and Aliyev discussed the possibility of Israel receiving oil from Azerbaijan via the Ceyhan pipeline, when and if it is completed. The oil would be carried to Israel by means of a pipeline under the Mediterranean Sea from Ceyhan to Haifa by-passing the Syrian land route.

Tehran immediately blasted Aliyev for agreeing to talk to Netanyahu.

---

[112]For an appreciation of Iran's wider foreign policy since the revolution in 1979 see Anushiravan Ehteshami, *After Khomeini:The Iranian Second Republic* (New York: Routledge, 1995), 126-96.

Tehran radio announced that Baku "has been playing a dangerous game by receiving the Zionist regime's expansionist prime minister. By doing this it has destabilized its own ties with Islamic states in the region and the world. It is probable that if such efforts continue, the Islamic people of Azerbaijan will eventually be pushed to react in a bid to pressure the government to break its ties with the Zionists, as people have done in Turkey and Egypt."[113]

By 16 September, Iran had stepped up its attacks on Baku. Kemal Kharrazi, Iran's foreign minister, stated that "Israel's relations with Azerbaijan were unacceptable to Iran." He emphasized specifically Israel's cooperation with Azerbaijan in the field of intelligence operations. Kharrazi stressed, "We are naturally considering the presence of the Zionist regime in such countries as Azerbaijan and Turkey and cooperation among them as against our national interests. We are not pleased with all of this. It is our natural right to be concerned about such developments. We think that this is not in the interest of the region that the Israeli regime would want to be present in this region."[114]

It is obvious from the above that the last thing that Iran wants is Israeli meddling in Azerbaijan and in its own Azeri question. This would be the reverse of Israel's support for the Kurds in Iraq during the 1960s and early 1970s. Indeed, if Tehran judges that Azerbaijan's relations with Israel continue to strengthen, it might well seek to undermine the Aliyev government. Tehran's opposition to increased Baku-Tel Aviv relations makes its opposition to the Turkey-Israel-U.S. alliances pale in comparison.

Iran also does not want Turkey to use the Kurdish question in order to minimize its role in being able to participate in the sharing and management of the oil and gas resources of the Caspian Sea region and in the pipeline distribution network to transport the energy resources. Iran needs desperately to share in the distribution of the oil and gas of the Caspian Sea region and Central Asia in order to strengthen the regime's status. By achieving and maintaining such policies Iran lessens the abilities of the U.S. and Europe to isolate it further via diplomatic or economic means. It also allows Iran to play the U.S. against Europe, as the Mykonos verdict revealed. The EU countries broke diplomatic

---

[113]*TRKNWS-L*, 1 September 1997.

[114]*TRKNWS-L*, 16 September 1997.

relations with Iran after the Mykonos verdict, but the U.S. gave its consent for the completion of the gas pipeline from Turkmenistan to Turkey via Iran. The U.S. did so despite its 1996 economic sanctions against Tehran. One of the reasons for the U.S. dispensation was its realization that its strong ally, Turkey, is desperately in need of energy resources. The U.S. government also realizes that the pipeline, and others to follow it, which traverses either northern Iran or eastern or southeastern Turkey, compels Ankara and Tehran to cooperate against the PKK and other Kurdish nationalist groups or, indeed, terrorist groups, who might want to sabotage such pipelines. In the 1990s Turkey's need for energy provided Iran with an opportunity to lessen its isolation and increase its usefulness to the U.S. and international capitalism. These developments also contributed further to the unraveling of the post-Gulf war strategy to encourage a strong Kurdish entity in northern Iraq. It also eases Turkey's and Iran's suspicions that in the wake of the Persian Gulf war the U.S. and Europe wanted to see, over a respectable period of time, the emergence of a Kurdish state in northern Iraq, much like Israel emerged in the twentieth century. This is a development that Iran will not want to miss, despite the negative effects it will have on the Iranian regime's rhetoric that the Islamic revolution in Iran provides an alternative to third world revolutionary movements built on socialist or nationalist discourse.[115] This is a position that will likely be pursued vigorously by President Mohammad Khatami.

Iran does not want the Kurdish question to affect its strategic economic polices and its relations with Turkey, and this study shows that Tehran has not allowed it to do so. This said, it is important to note that Iran's relations with Turkey after the revolution have not been as "warm and close" as Anushiravan Ehteshami suggests, at least with regards to the Kurdish question. They have been cooperative, however, on the geopolitical and geostrategical levels.[116] In July 1989 when Turkey expelled Iran's ambassador for meddling in its internal affairs, Hojjatolislam Hashemi Rafsanjani, prior to his election as President of Iran, had already stated his conviction that there "existed direct linkage between economic prosperity at home and political stability in the Persian Gulf...trust among neighbors and a calm situation in the region can

---

[115]*Ibid.*

[116]*Ibid.*

automatically solve many problems for us [my italics]."[117]   During his eight-year presidency (1989-97) Tehran pursued this policy, especially with regard to its relations with Turkey and to the Kurdish question.

One must place Iran's economic policies in proper perspective. In 1989, although less in the 1990s, the main trading partners of Iran were still non-Muslim countries. In 1989, out of some twenty of Iran's major trading partners, there was only one Muslim country, and, significantly, it was Turkey, which ranked ninth among Iran's trading partners. Iran's exports to Turkey came to 4.5 percent of its total exports, and its imports from Turkey were 7.0 percent of the total. Imports from Turkey ranked third behind only Japan and Germany.[118]   By 1992 Iran's exports to Turkey of $325 million and imports of $402 million had declined considerably from the high point of 1985, but by 1997 they were back to $1 billion and estimated to reach $2 billion by the year 2,000. The completion of the gas pipeline from Turkmenistan in 1998 would seem to indicate that this goal will be reached and probably surpassed. In spite of the decline in trade from 1985 onward, Iran invested in Turkey more than any other Muslim country. The number of foreign companies with Iranian capital operating in Turkey was 43 in 1986; 88 in 1987; 134 in 1988; 167 in 1989; 183 in 1990; 192 in 1991; and 202 in 1992.[119] The number by 1998 will likely be much higher. It must also be taken into account that during the last 20 years, the 1.5 million Iranians in Turkey are establishing businesses much like the Iranian diaspora in the U.S. and France and the Turkish diaspora in Germany. Many of these businesses will continued to draw capital from Iran through both official and unofficial channels.

Iran does not want Turkey to expand or to further consolidate its position in northern Iraq on a permanent basis. By doing so, Ankara would be in a position to be a significant player in Persian Gulf politics. Indeed, by its closer presence to the Gulf it would become a player in Persian Gulf politics, its role similar to that which Israel plays in spite of its distance from the Persian Gulf. Turkey would be much closer. Tehran also does not want to see Turkey dominate completely the Kurdish

---

[117]*Ibid.* 146.

[118]*Ibid.* 213.

[119]İhsan Gürkan, "Turkish-Iranian Relations: Dynamics in Continuity and Change," *Turkish Review of Middle East Studies*, vol. 7 (1993):63.

nationalist organizations in Iraq and through them to dominate the politics of northern Iraq, hence becoming an even stronger force in the politics of Iraq. This fear makes Iran support the PUK and the PKK, and the latter both in Iraq and in northern Iran. Lastly, a strong Turkish presence in Iraq, whether via Turkish armed forces or the Kurdish organizations, also threatens to influence the Azeri question.

This is why Iran has raised such a hue and cry over the Turkey-Israel alliance that became more manifest in 1996. While the Turkey-Israel alliance has many dimensions, it bears also on Turkey-Iran relations in that the alliance threatens Syria, Iran's major Arab ally, by attempting to compel Damascus to accept American and Israeli dictates in the "peace process." By allying with Israel, Turkey hopes to use Israel's clout and that of its supporters in the U.S. to compel Syria to stop sheltering and supporting the PKK within Syria, Iraq and Iran and elsewhere in the Middle East and Europe. Such a development would greatly weaken Syria's ability to play the Kurdish card against Turkey. Syria employs the Kurdish card not only as a lever to extract greater water resources from the Euphrates but also because it realizes that the Kurdish nationalist movement in general, and not just the PKK, is the paramount problem confronting Turkey. Supporting the PKK and Kurdish nationalism in Turkey serves to weaken the Turkish state, and Damascus hopes no doubt mightily so. It must be remembered that many of the leaders and commanders of the PKK in Turkey during the 1980s and 1990s have been Kurds from Syria. Supporting the PKK also reduces the possibility of a stronger Kurdish nationalist movement in Syria. By supporting PKK operations in Turkey and elsewhere, Damascus, much like Turkey itself in its relations with Iran with regard to the Kurdish question, hopes to externalize an internal problem.

If Turkey, Israel, and by extension, the U.S., force Syria to abandon its Kurdish card, it would be vulnerable to all kinds of other Turkish, Israeli and American demands. Syria's usefulness to Iran, especially concerning its relations with Turkey, would be substantially diminished. It would not be able to cooperate with Iran in opposing Turkish policies in northern Iraq, thus removing an important cushion in Iran-Turkish relations that could result in more direct, and possibly even heightened, confrontation. Iran knows how skillfully Israel used the Kurdish card against it in the 1960s and 1970s and it does not intend the same card to be played in reverse.[120] The Turkey-Israel alliance has the potential to reduce Syria's

---

[120]Jonathan C. Randall, *After Such Knowledge, What Forgiveness* (New York:

ability to continue to carry out a relatively independent foreign policy as a middle level regional power by compelling it to accept Tel Aviv's, Washington's and now Ankara's dictates. Iranian support for Syria is an important prophylactic to prevent that from that happening. In spite of Tehran's deep concerns regarding the Israel-Turkey alliance, the naval maneuvers among Turkey, Israel and the U.S. orginally scheduled for mid October and then postponed because of the outcry from Arab countries, and Ankara's hostile relations with its Syrian ally, Kemal Kharrazi, Iran's foreign minister, continued to call for better relations with Turkey throughout September 1997 and suggested that the two countries should return their ambassadors to their posts. Kharrazi was as good as his word. On 22 September while attending meetings of the UN in New York, he and Turkish Foreign Minister Ismail Cem agreed that ambassadors would be returned to their posts. In early December 1997, Ankara and Tehran announced that their   ambassadors would return to their respective posts in early 1998. It is indictive of the differences between Turkey   and Iran that EU ambassadors returned to Tehran and Iranian   ambassadors to the EU countries before Ankara and Tehran once again exchanged ambassadors.

The Kurdish Question and Its Effects on Turkey's Geopolitical and Geostrategical Concerns in the 1990s

Turkey does not want the trans-state Kurdish question and its monumental Kurdish problem to affect its wider geopolitic and geostrategic relationship with Iran. Turkey's greatest need is for energy resources. Its rapid industrialization and its burgeoning population make energy its second greatest challenge. Ankara's need for energy demands cooperation, even if the cooperation is competitive in many areas with Iran. It wants to share and participate in the oil and gas resources of the Caspian Sea region and in Central Asia. Turkey's need for gas and oil is much greater than Iran's. Tehran's need is to sell its oil and gas and to participate in the distribution of the gas and oil of the Caspian basin and Central Asia. Turkey has to make sure that it does not antagonize Iran unnecessarily in these regions, especially in Azerbaijan. Iran is willing to have friendly

---

Farrar, Straus and Geroux, 1997) is the most recent and best account of Israel's activities among the Kurds in Iraq and Iran during this period, especially pages 184-201.

cooperation but not hostile unilateralism on the part of Turkey in alliance with the U.S., Europe or Israel. This means that in no way should Ankara encourage Azerbaijani or Azeri nationalism. Tehran does not want a repeat of Turkey's support for Azerbaijani nationalism that characterized Abufez Elchibey's policies while he was President of Azerbaijan from 1991 to 1993 before being overthrown in a coup and replaced by Haidar Aliyev.[121] While Iran did encourage the overthrow of Elchibey, it did not, as far as I know, participate directly in the actions that led to his overthrow, unlike Turkey, which participated directly in the attempt to overthrow Aliyev soon after he came to power. Tansu Çiller, then the Turkish prime minister, was later accused of supplying a government plane to fly some of the conspirators from Turkey to Baku.[122]

Turkey's policy toward Azerbaijan during the presidency of Elchibey is a good example of policies that Tehran finds unacceptable. In response to Turkey's aggressive polices, Tehran strengthened relations with Armenia and did little to resolve the conflict between Yerevan and Baku. After Aliyev came to power and even after Turkey's probable participation in a coup to overthrow him, Aliyev sought better relations with both countries in appreciation of their geopolitical and geostrategical concerns in the region.

Because of its energy needs, Turkey also seeks to prevent Iran-Russian cooperation which would jeopardize its access to the oil and gas in the Caspian Sea region and Central Asia, especially in Turkmenistan and Kazakhstan. Moscow has used and threatens to use the Kurdish card if Turkey pursues too aggressive a policy in the Caucasus, such as it did in Chechnya. When Turkey supplied arms and soldiers to the Chechens, Moscow gave almost official recognition to the PKK in Russia and the CIS.[123] A simultaneous use of the Kurdish card by Moscow and Tehran would be deadly for Turkey. While Ankara pursues a policy to lessen the possibilities of either Moscow or Tehran from too forcefully using the Kurdish card, it is in a better position to assure that Iran does not pursue such a policy than it is to prevent Russia from using it.

---

[121]Robert Olson, "The Kurdish Question and Chechnya: Turkey versus Russia," *Middle East Policy*, vol. iv, no. 3 (1996):117-8.

[122]Robert Olson, "The Rose of Istanbul," *Middle East International*, no. 556, 8 August, 1997, 4; *Hürriyet*, 24 July 1997. The charges were made by Doğu Perinçek, the leader of the Workers' Party.

[123]*Ibid*.

Both Iran and Turkey realize that cooperation with each other in sharing and participating in the oil and gas resources of the Caspian Sea basin and Central Asia is in their interests as it lessens Russian influence in those countries. The less the Russian influence in the Caucasus and Central Asia, the stronger become both Turkey's and Iran's positions.

Iran's ability to influence Turkey's policy in the eastern Mediterranean with regard to the Kurdish question is less than in adjacent regions. As discussed above, Iran has attempted to contain Turkey by allying with Syria, Greece and the Greek Republic of Cyprus. But Tehran does not want by its alliance with Syria to lead Turkey to think that it threatens its geopolitical interests in the Aegean Sea or the eastern Mediterranean, which are more vital to Turkey than its interests in the Caucasus and Central Asia. Other than the challenge from the Kurds, the most important concern of Turkey is to maintain its geopolitical strength in the Aegean vis à vis Greece and in the eastern Mediterranean, including Cyprus. For example, if Iran were to sell missiles to the Greek Cypriots, as Russia did in January 1997 (as of November 1997 the missiles still not not reached Cyprus), Ankara's response to Iran would be much stronger than its response to Russia; it might even be cause for war. As mentioned above, Mesut Yılmaz, before he became prime minister in June 1997, declared that if Iran were found to have supplied the missiles that shot down two Turkish helicopters over northern Iraq, it would be cause for war. At first glance, it would seem that Iran would have more capabilities to pursue anti-Turkish policies in the eastern Mediterranean than in the Caucasus or northern Iraq, but because of the vulnerability of Iran in its wider relations with Turkey in the Caucasus, Central Asia and Azerbaijan, it cannot do so. Ankara thinks that Tehran's eastern Mediterranean behavior, including its alliance with Syria, can be moderated by its vulnerabilities in the Middle East, Caucasus, Caspian Sea region and Central Asia. There is a much closer connection between both countries' eastern Mediterranean and Caucasus-Central Asia policies than most analysts realize. The one area in which both countries have some maneuverability is in northern Iraq, and that is the reason the jockeying for position and power there is more vigorous.

Conclusion

This study demonstrates the great continuity in Iranian-Turkish relations with regard to the Kurdish question from the imperial centuries through the post-WW I establishment of national states to the present. This is remarkable given that not only did the Turkish portions of the Ottoman empire and the Qajar empire transform themselves into national states, they did so among vicissitudes and profound challenges and, in the case of the Turkey, with great shrinkage of territory. In the post-WW I era, neither country allowed Kurdish nationalist movements to challenge the Turkish and Iranian ethnic-based nationalism that each regime tried to implement. The challenge of the 1920s and the 1990s in Turkey and in 1945-46 and 1979-83 in Iran were not successful in challenging the territorial base or the ethnic-based nationalist discourse of the majoritarian ethnic group, although Iran's state nationalist discourse was less Iranian ethnic-based after the Islamic revolution in 1979. By the 1990s the Kemalist elite's Turkish-based ethnic nationalism was also beginning to whither under the daily barrage of Kurdish demands, although as this study was being written it had not yet given way. But it was clear by the end of 1997 that the demands of Kurdish nationalism cannot much longer be contained in Turkey, even by means of massive repression.

This study suggests that the major need of Turkey and Iran to manage the Kurdish question were/are the challenges that it presents to their wider interests. This conclusion confirms the thesis established at the beginning of this study that "omni-balancing" is the best international relations model to explain each country's foreign policy behavior as far as the trans-state Kurdish question is concerned. Omni-balancing emphasizes that where external threats are significant and internal ones manageable, priority may tilt toward external threats. This has been the paradigm followed with regard to the Kurdish question in Turkey-Iran relations since WW I. The internal threat of the Kurdish problem, i.e., the challenge of Kurdish nationalism to the Turkish state in its configuration since 1923 to the end of 1997, however, modifies the omni-balancing paradigm.[124]

Omni-balancing can be construed to include three international relations theories: the "rational actor," the "irrational actor," and the "capital accumulator," in that they represent three implicit survival requisites that potentially shape policy: geopolitically shaped national interests (ambitions) and external threats; domestic politics and internal ideological legitimization needs; and economic needs. Anushiravan Ehteshami and Raymond Hinnebusch state: "In any given regime and at

---

[124]My characterization of omni-balancing here, as at the beginning of the study, follows that of Ehteshami and Hinnebusch, 19-20.

any given time, threats to one or the other may be dominant in decision-makers' calculations, although in the long run if any are neglected, regime stability is put to risk."[125] This study validates these assertions. The two authors also suggest that "the notion of omni-balancing could also be extended by taking rationality [of the neorealist school] to mean attending not only to security threats [both internal and external] but also to capital accumulation and rent acquisition requisites. Since these various requisites of state-formation may conflict in any given situation, and no policy is therefore likely to appear fully rational from all points of view, the highest rationality may be the ability to make a reasonable series of trade-offs." This paradigm very much fits the analysis of the Kurdish question in its trans-state dimensions and the Kurdish problem in its domestic manifestations as a threat in Turkish and Iranian relations.

The geopolitical and geostrategical concerns of both Turkey and Iran in the 1990s are clearly associated with their economic needs. These economic needs have compelled them to seek accommodation in the geopolitical arena in order that such accommodation would/will prevent or lessen the desire of either state to try to use the Kurdish card in order to jeopardize the regimes in power by attempting to influence each country's respective Kurdish nationalist movement in order to challenge the obtaining domestic political structure and the internal ideological legitimization upon which each depends to survive. Perhaps this aspect of the omni-balancing model is best characterized by the headlines in Turkish and Iranian newspaper on 4 August 1997. Analyzing President Mohammad Khatami's inaugural speech, the Iranian newpapers said that it devoted "ten percent to foreign policy and fifteen percent to economic policy." On the same day Turkish newspapers announced that Turkey hoped to increase its exports from the expected amount of $33 billion in 1997 to $50 billion by the year 2,000.[126]

The omni-balancing model suggests that if Turkey and Iran want to remain middle level ranking powers in a penetrated region, they will find it in their interests to continue to manage the Kurdish question so that it does not threaten their wider geopolitical, geostrategical and economic interests. They must coordinate the management of their geopolitical and geostrategical concerns with the management of their own domestic

---

[125]*Ibid.* 19.

[126]*Iran Times*, 4 August 1997; *Hürriyet*, 4 August 1997.

Kurdish problems so that the former does not adversely affect the latter. This is especially true in the case of Turkey. Not to do so could jeopardize the middle level power ranking that each country has assiduously pursued.

BIBLIOGRAPHY

Afrasiabi, K. L. *After Khomeini: New Directions in Iran's Foreign Policy*. Boulder: Westview Press, 1994.

Abramowitz, Morton L. "Dateline Ankara: Turkey After Ozal." *Foreign Policy*, no. 91 (Summer 1993):164-85.

Ahmad, Feroz. *The Making of Modern Turkey*. London: Routledge, 1993.

Akdoğan, Selim M. *36. Paralel ve Ortadoğu*. İstanbul: Nubihar Yayınları, 1995.

Amuzegar, Jahangir. *Iran's Economy under the Islamic Republic*. New York: I. B. Tauris, 1993.

Amirahmadi, Hooshang. *Revolution and Economic Transition: The Iranian Experience*. Albany: State University of New York Press, 1990.

Anderson, Benedict. *Imagined Communities*. New York: Verso, 1991.

Andrews, Peter A. ed. *Ethnic Groups in the Republic of Turkey*. Wiesbaden: Dr. Ludwig Reichert Verlag, 1989.

Anter, Musa. *Hatırlarım*. İstanbul: Yön Yayıncılık, 1991.

Atabaki, Touraj. *Azerbaijan: Ethnicity and Autonomy in in Twenieth Century Iran*. New York: British Academy Press, 1993.

Aydin, Ahmet. *Kürtler, PKK ve A. Öcalan*. (No publication data).

Aykan, Mamut Bali. "Turkey's Policy in Northern Iraq, 1991-95." *Middle East Studies*, vol. 32, no. 4 (1996):343-66.

_____. "Turkish Perspectives on Turkish-US Relations Concerning Persian Gulf Security in the Post-Cold War Era: 1989-1995." *Middle East Journal*, vol. 50, no. 3 (1996):344-58.

Aytar, Osman. *Kürdün "Maküs Talih" i ve "Güneydoğu" Anadolu Projesi*. İstanbul: Medya Güneşi Yayınları, 1991.

Ballı, Raffet. *Kürt Dosyası*. İstanbul: Cem Yayınları, 1991.

Barkey, Henri J. *Reluctant Neighbor: Turkey's Role in the Middle East*. Washington, D.C.: United States Institute of Peace Press, 1996.

_____. "Turkey's Kurdish Dilemma." *Survival*, vol. 35, no. 4 (1993):51-70.

_____. "The Silent Victor: Turkey's Role in the Gulf War," in Efraim Karsh, ed. *The Iran-Iraq War: Impact and Implications*, 133-53. New York: St. Martin's Press, 1989.

____. "Turkish-American Relations in the Post-War Era: An alliance of convenience." *Orient*, vol. 33, no. 3 (1992):447-64.

____. "Under the Gun: Turkish Foreign Policy and the Kurdish Question," in Robert Olson, ed. *The Turkish Nationalist Movement in the 1990s: Its Impact on Turkey and the Middle East*, 65-83. Lexington: University Press of Kentucky.

Barkey, Henri and Graham E. Fuller. "Turkey's Kurdish Question and Missed Opportunities." *Middle East Journal*, vol. 51, no. 1 (1997):59-79.

Barzin, Saeed. "Bitter Fruit of Mykonos." *Middle East International*, no. 548 (18 April 1997).

Başkaya, Fikret. *Paradigmanın İflası: Resmi İdeolojinin Eleştirisine Giriş*. İstanbul: Doz Basım, 1991.

Bayrak, Mehmet. *Kürtler ve Ulusal-Demokratik Mücadeleleri*. Ankara: Öz-Ge Yayınları, 1993.

Beşikçi, İsmail. *Kürdistan Üzerinde Emperyalist Bölüşüm Mücadelesi, 1915-1925*. İstanbul: Yurt Kitap, 1992.

____. *Kürtlerin Mecburi İskan*. Ankara: Yurt Kitap Yayın, 1991.

____. *Tunceli Kanunu (1935) ve Dersim Jenosidi*. İstanbul: Belge Yayınları, 1990.

____. *Ortadoğu'da Devlet Terörü*. İstanbul: Yurt Kitap, 1991.

____. Birand, Mehmet Ali. *Apo ve PKK*. İstanbul: Milliyet Yayınları, 1992.

Bolukbasi, Suha. "Ankara's Baku Centered Transcaucasia Policy: Has It Failed?" *Middle East Journal*, no. 51, no. 1 (1997):80-94.

____. "Ankara, Damascus, Baghdad and the Regionalization of Turkey's Kurdish Secessionism." *Journal of South Asian and Middle Eastern Studies*, vol. 14, no. 4 (1993):15-36.

____. "Turkey Copes with Revolutionary Iran." *Journal of South Asian and Middle Eastern Studies*, vol. 13, no. 1 & 2 (1989):94-109.

Bozarslan, Hamit. "Einige Bemerkungen Zur Entwicklung des Kurden Problems in der Zwischen Kriegzeit," in Alfred Janata, ed. *Kurden Azadi: Freiheit in Den Bergen*, 114-27. Schallaburg: 1992.

____. "Etats et Modes de Gestion du Problème Kurde." *Peuples Méditeranéens*, nos. 68-69 (1994):185-214.

____. "Le Kemalisme et le problém kurde," in H. Hakim, ed. *Les Kurdes par Dela l'Exode*, 63-89. Paris: Éditions L'Harmattan, 1992.

____. "The Kurdish Question in Turkish Political Life: The Situation as of 1990," in Turaj Atabaki and Margeet Darleijin, eds. *Kurdistan in Search of Ethnic Identity*, 1-23. Utrecht: University of Utrecht, 1990.

———. "Political Aspects of the Kurdish Problem in Contemporary Turkey," in Philip G. Kreyenbroek and Stefan Sperl, eds. *The Kurds: A Contemporary Survey*, 95-114. London: Routledge, 1992.

———. "Political Aspects and the Kurdish Issue in Turkey," in Robert Olson, ed. *The Kurdish Nationalist Movement in Turkey in the 1990s: Its Impact on Turkey and the Middle East*, 135-53. Lexington: University Press of Kentucky, 1996.

Bruinessen, Martin van. *Agha, Shaikh and State: The Social and Political Structure of Kurdistan*. London: Zed Books, Ltd., 1992.

———. *Evliya Çelebi in Diyarbekir*. Leiden: E. J. Brill, 1988.

———. "Between Guerrilla War and Political Murder: The Workers' Party of Kurdistan." *Middle East Report*, no. 153 (July-August 1988):40-42, 44-46, 50.

———. "Genocide in Kurdistan?: The Suppression of the Dersim Rebellion in Turkey (1937-38) and the Chemical War Against the Iraqi Kurds (1988)," in George Andreopulus, ed. *Genocide: Conceptual and Historical Dimensions*, 141-70. Philadelphia: University of Pennsylvania Press, 1994.

———. "Kurdish Tribes and the State of Iran: The Case of Simko's Revolt," in Richard Tapper, ed. *The Conflict of Tribe and State in Iran and Afghanistan*, 364-400. London: Croom-Helm, 1983

———. *Kürdistan Üzerine Yazılar*. İstanbul: İletişim Yayınları, 1993.

———. "Nationalisme kurde et ethnicité intra-kurde." *Peuples Méditerranéens*, nos. 68-69 (1994):11-38.

———. "The Kurds in Turkey: Further Restrictions on Basic Rights." *International Commission of Jurists: The Review*, no. 45 (1990):46-52.

———. "Turkey's Death Squads." *Middle East Report*, no. 199 (April-June 1996): 20-25.

Burkay, Kemal. *Geçmişten Bugüne: Kürtler ve Kürdistan*. İstanbul: Deng Yayınları, 1992.

Chaliand, Gerard, ed. *A People without a Country: The Kurds and Kurdistan*. New York: Olive Branch Press, 1993.

Chehabi, H. E. "Ardabil Becomes a Province: Center-Periphery Relations in Iran." *International Journal of Middle East Studies*, vol. 29, no. 2 (1997):235-53.

Criss, Nur Bilge. "The Nature of PKK Terrorism in Turkey." *Studies in*

Conflict & Terrorism, vol. 18, no. 1 (1995):17-37.

Dankoff, Robert. The Intimate Life of an Ottoman Statesman: Melek Ahmet Paşa as Portrayed in Evliya Çelebi's Book of Travels. Albany: State University of New York, 1991.

David, Steven R. "Explaining Third World Alignment." World Politics, vol. 43, no. 2 (1991):233-57.

Dersimi, Nuri M. Kürdistan Tarihinde Dersim. Aleppo: Ani Matbaası, 1952.

Dunn, Michael Collins."The Kurdish 'Question': Is there an Answer?" Middle East Policy, vol. 4, no. 3 (1995):72-86.

Ergil, Doğu. Güney Doğu Raporu. İstanbul: Hürriyet Yayınları, 1995.

Entessar, Nader. Kurdish Ethnonationalism. Boulder: Lynne Rienner Publishers, 1992.

_____. "Kurdish Conflict in a Regional Perspective," in M. E. Ahrari, ed. Change and Continuity in the Middle East: Conflict Resolution and Prospects for Peace, 47-73. New York: St. Martin's, 1996.

Ehteshami, Anoushiravan. After Khomeini: The Iranian Second Republic. New York: Routledge, 1995.

_____ and Raymond A. Hinnebusch. Syria and Iran: Middle Powers in a Penetrated Regional System. New York: Routledge, 1997.

Fuller, Graham E. "Conclusions: The Growing Role of Turkey in the World, Graham E. Fuller and Iran Lesser, eds. Turkey's New Geopolitics: From the Balkans to Western China, 163-84. Boulder: Westview Press, 1993.

_____. Iraq in the Next Decade: Will Iran Survive until 2002? Santa Monica: Rand Corporation, 1992.

_____. "The Fate of the Kurds." Foreign Affairs, vol. 72, no. 2 (1993):108-21.

_____. "Turkey's New Eastern Orientation," in Graham E. Fuller and Ian O. Lesser, eds. Turkey's New Geopolitics: From the Balkans to Western China, 37-98. Boulder: Westview Press, 1993.

Göle, Nilüfer. "Secularism and Islamism in Turkey: The Making of Elites and Counter-elites." Middle East Journal, vol. 51, no. 1 (1997):46-58.

_____. "Authoritarianism and Islamist Politics: The Case of Turkey," in Augustus Richard Norton, ed. Civil Society in the Middle East, vol. 2:17-43. New York: E. J. Brill, 1996.

_____. "Engineers: Technocratic Democracy," in Metin Heper, Ayşe Öncü and Heinz Kramer, eds. Turkey and the West: Changing Political and Cultural Identities, 199-218. London: I. B. Tauris, 1993.

_____. "Entre Le "Gauchisme" et L'"Islamisme": L'Émergence de L'Idéologie Techniciste en Turquie," in Elizaeth Longuenesse, ed. *Bâtisseurs et Bureaucrats: Ingénieurs et Société au Maghreb et au Moyen-Orient*, 309-21. Paris: Centre National de la Recherche Scientifique, 1990.

_____. "Ingénieurs islamistes et étudiantes voilées en Turquie: entre le totalitarisme et l'individualisme," in Gilles Kepel and Yann Richard, eds. *Intellectuels et Militants de l'Islam Contemporain*, 167-90. Paris: Éditions du Seuil, 1990.

Gürbey, Gülistan. "Autonomie-option zer friedlichen Beilegung des Kurdenkonfliktes in der Turkei?" in *Hessische Stiftung Friedens und Konflict Forschung*. Report 5 (1997), 1-46.

_____. "The Development of the Kurdish Nationalism Movement in Turkey Since the 1990s," in Robert Olson, ed. *The Kurdish Nationalist Movement in the 1990s: Its Impact on Turkey and the Middle East*, 9-37. Lexington: University Press of Kentucky, 1996.

Gürkan, İhsan. "Turkey's Relations with Iran." *Turkish Review of Middle East Studies*, vol. 7 (1993):59-98.

Gunter, Michael M. *The Kurds in Turkey: A Political Dilemma*. Boulder: Westview Press, 1990.

_____. *The Kurds of Iraq: Tragedy and Hope*. New York: St. Martin's Press, 1992.

_____. *The Kurds and the Future of Turkey*. New York: St. Martin's Press, 1997.

_____. "A *de facto* Kurdish State in Northern Iraq." *Third World Quarterly*. vol. 14, no. 2 (1993):295-319.

_____. "The Iraqi National Congress (INC) and the Future of the Iraqi Opposition." *Journal of South Asian and Middle Eastern Studies*, vol. 19, no. 3 (1996):1-20.

_____. "The Kurdish Problem in Turkey." *Middle East Journal*, vol. 42, no. 3 (1988): 389-406.

_____. "Turkey and the Kurds: New Developments in 1991." *Journal of South Asian and Middle Eastern Studies*, vol. 15, no. 2 (1991):32-45.

_____. "The Kurdish Insurgency in Turkey." *Journal of South Asian and Middle Eastern Studies*, vol. 13, no. 2 (1990):57-81.

_____. "The KDP-PUK Conflict in Northern Iraq." *Middle East Journal*, vol. 50, no. 2 (1996):225-41.

_____. "Kurdish Infighting: The PKK-KDP Conflict," in Robert Olson, ed.

The Kurdish Nationalist Movement in the 1990s: Its Impact on Turkey and the Middle East, 50-62. Lexington: University Press of Kentucky, 1996.

Gurr, Ted R. *Minorities at Risk: A Global View of Ethnopolitical Conflict*. Washington, D.C.: United States Institute of Peace, 1993.

İpekçi, Abdi. *İnönü Atatürk Anlatıyor*. İstanbul: Am Yayın Evi, 1981.

Jansen, Michael. "Asad on Tour." *Middle East International*, no. 556 (8 August 1997).

Jwaideh, Wadie. *The Kurdish Nationalist Movement: Its Origins and Developments*. University of Syracuse, unpublished Ph. D. Dissertation, 1960.

Hale, William. *Turkish Politics and the Military*. London: Routledge, 1994.

Halliday, Fred. "The Gulf War and its aftermath." *International Affairs*, vol. 67, no. 2 (1991):223-34.

Heper, Metin. "Islam and Democracy in Turkey: Toward a Reconcilation?" *Middle East Journal*, vol. 51, no. 1 (1997):32-45.

_____ and Aylin Güney. "The Military and Democracy in the Third Turkish Republic." *Armed Forces & Society*, vol. 22, no. 4 (1996): 619-42.

Hiro, Dilip. "Why is the US Inflating Caspian Oil Reserves?" *Middle East International* (12 September 1997).

Hurewitz, J. C. *Diplomacy in the Near and Middle East: A Documentary Record: 1535-1914*, vol. 1 & 2. New York: D. van Nostrand Company, Inc., 1956.

Kadıoğlu, Ayşe. "The Paradox of Turkish Nationalism and the Construction of Offical Identity." *Middle Eastern Studies*, no. 32, no. 2 (1996):177-93.

Karpat, Kemal H. ed. *Turkish Foriegn Policy: Recent Developments*. Madison: University of Wisconsin Press, 1996.

Kazemi, Farhad. "Civil Society and Iranian Politics," in Richard Augustus Norton, ed. *Civil Society in the Middle East*:119-52. New York: E. J. Brill, 1996.

Keohane, Robert O. *Neorealism and Its Critics*. New York: Columbia University Press, 1986.

Kieser, Hans Lukas. "L'Alévisme Kurde," in *Peuples Méditerranées*, nos. 68-69 (1994):57-76.

Kirişci, Kemal and Gareth M. Winrow. *Kürt Sorunu: Kökeni ve Gelişimi.*

İstanbul: Numune Matbaacılık, 1997.

_____. *The Kurdish Question and Turkey: An Example of a Trans-State Ethnic Conflict*. London: Frank Cass, 1997.

Kirişci, Kemal. "Turkey and the Kurdish Safe-Haven in Northern Iraq." *Journal of South Asian and Middle Eastern Studies*, vol. 19, no. 3 (1996):21-39.

Kreyenbroek, Philip G. and Stefan Sperl, eds. *The Kurds: A Contemporary Overview*. London: Routledge, 1992.

Küçük, Yalçin. *Kürtler Üzerine Tezler*. İstanbul: Dönem Yayıncılık, 1990.

Lawson, Fred. *Why Syria Goes to War: Thirty Years of Confrontation*, Ithaca: Cornell University Press, 1996.

Laizer, Sheri. *Martyrs, Traitors and Patriots: Kurdistan after the Gulf War*. London: Zed Books, 1996.

Makovsky, Alan, "Israeli-Turkish Relations: A Turkish "Periphery Strategy"? in Henri J. Barkey, ed. *Reluctant Neighbor: Turkey's Role in the Middle East*, 147-70. Washinton, D.C.: United States Institute of Peace Press, 1996

McDowall, David. *The Kurds: A Nation Denied*. London: Minority Rights Publications, 1992.

_____. *A Modern History of the Kurds*. London: I.B. Tauris, 1996.

_____. "The Kurdish Question in the 1990s," in *Peuples Méditeranéens*, nos. 68-69 (1994):243-66.

McLachlan, Keith ed. *The Boundaries of Modern Iran*. New York: St. Martin's Press, 1994.

Muller, Mark. "Nationalism and the Rule of Law in Turkey: The Elimination of Kurdish Representation During the 1990s," in Robert Olson, ed. *The Kurdish Nationalist Movement in the 1990s: Its Impact on Turkey and the Middle East*, 173-199. Lexington: University Press of Kentucky, 1996.

Mumcu, Uğur. *Kürt İslam Ayaklanması, 1919-1925*. İstanbul: Tekin Yayınevi, 1991.

_____. *Kürt Dosyası*. İstanbul: Tekin Yayınevi, 1994.

Mutlu, Servet. "Ethnic Kurds in Turkey: A Demographic Study." *International Journal of Middle East Studies*, vol. 28, no. 4 (1996):517-41.

_____. "The Southeastern Anatolia Project (GAP) of Turkey: Its Context, Objectives and Prospects." *Orient*, vol. 37, no. 1 (1996):59-86.

Olson, Robert. *The Siege of Mosul and Ottoman-Persian Relations, 1718-1743: A Study of Rebellion in the Capital and War in the*

Provinces of the Ottoman Empire. Bloomington: Indiana University Press, 1975.

_____. *The Emergence of Kurdish Nationalism and the Sheikh Said Rebellion: 1880-1925*. Austin: University of Texas Press, 1989.

_____. *Kürt Milliyetçiliğinin Kaynakları ve Şeyh Said İsyanı* (Turkish translation of above book). İstanbul: Öz-Ge Yayınları, 1992.

_____. *Imperial Meanderings and Republican By-Ways: Essays on Eighteenth Century Ottoman and Twentieth Century History of Turkey*. İstanbul:Isis Press, 1996.

_____. ed. *The Kurdish Nationalist Movement in the 1990s: Its Impact on Turkey and the Middle East*. Lexington: University Press of Kentucky, 1996.

_____. "The Creation of a Kurdish State in the 1990's?" *Journal of South Asian and Middle Eastern Studies*, vol. 15, no. 4 (1992):1-25.

_____. "Kurds and Turks: Two Documents Concerning Kurdish Autonomy in 1922-1923." *Journal of South Asian and Middle Eastern Studies*, vol. 15, no. 2 (991):20-31.

_____. "Battle for Kurdistan: The Churchill-Cox Correspondence Regarding the Creation of the State of Iraq, 1921-1923. "*Kurdish Studies: An International Journal*, vol. 5, nos. 1 & 2 (1992):29-44.

_____. "Five Stages of Kurdish Nationalism: 1880-1980." *Journal of Muslim Minority Affairs*, vol. 12, no. 2 (1991):392-410.

_____. "The Kurdish Question in the Aftermath of the Gulf War: Geopolitical and Geostrategic Changes in the Middle East." *Third World Quarterly*, vol. 13, no. 3 (1992):475-99.

_____. "The Kurdish Question and the Kurdish Problem: Some Geopolitic and Geostrategic Comparisons." *Peuples Méditerranéens*, nos. 68-69 (1994):215-42.

_____. "The Kurdish Question Four Years On: The Policies of Turkey, Syria, Iran and Iraq." *Middle East Policy*, vol. 3, no. 3 (1994):136-44.

_____. "The Kurdish Question and Turkey's Foreign Policy, 1991-95: From the Gulf War to the Incursion into Iraq." *Journal of South Asian and Middle Eastern Studies*, vol. 11, no. 4 (1995):1-30.

_____. "The Impact of the Southeast Anatolia Project (GAP) on Kurdish Nationalism in Turkey." *International Journal of Kurdish Studies*, vol. 9, nos. 1 & 2 (1996):95-102.

_____. "The Kurdish Question and Chechnya: Turkish and Russian Foreign Policies since the Gulf War." *Middle East Policy*, vol. 4, no. 3 (1996):1-30.

____. "The Sheikh Said Rebellion: Its Impact on the Development of the Turkish Air Force." *The Journal of Kurdish Studies*, vol. 1, no. 1 (1996):77-83.

____. "Turkey-Syria Relations: Kurds and Water." *Middle East Policy*, vol. 5, no. 2 (1997):168-95.

____. "The Kurdish Question and Turkey's Foreign Policy Toward Syria, Iran, Russia and Iraq since the Gulf War," in Robert Olson, ed. *The Kurdish Nationalist Movement in the 1990s: Its Impact on Turkey and the Middle East*, 84-113. Lexington: University Press of Kentucky, 1996

____ and Yücel Bozdağlıoğlu. "The New Democracy Movement in Turkey: A Response to Liberal Capitalism and Kurdish Ethnonationalism," in Robert Olson, ed. *The Kurdish Nationalist Movement in the 1990s: Its Impact on Turkey and on the Middle East*, 154-172. Lexington: University Press of Kentucky, 1996.

____. "Green Light from Moscow." *Middle East International*, no. 498 (14 April 1995).

____. "The Spread of Kurdish Nationnalism: A New Stage of Development."*Middle East International*, no. 511 (20 October 1995).

____. "The Cost of the Turkey's War Against the PKK." *Middle East International*, no. 512 (3 November 1995).

____. "Kurds and Islamists in Turkey." *Middle East International*, no. 518 (2 February 1996).

____. "Ethnic Cleansing in Turkey." *Middle East International*, no. 523 (12 April, 1996).

____. "Turkey, Israel Agreement and the Kurdish Question." *Middle East International*, no. 526 (24 May 1996).

____. "An Israeli-Kurdish Conflict?" *Middle East International*, no. 529 (9 September 1996).

____. The Erbakan Government and the Kurdish Question." *Middle East International*, no. 533 (24 May 1996).

____. "Israel and the Kurds." *Middle East International*, no. 546 (21 February, 1996).

____. "Democratisation and the Kurds in Turkey." *Middle East International*, no. 545 (7 March 1997).

____. "Letter from Sivas." *Middle East International*, no. 547 (4 April 1997).

____. "Israel and Turkey: Consolidating Relations." *Middle East*

International, no. 547 (4 April 1997).

_____. "The Rose of Istanbul." *Middle East International*, no. 556 (8 August, 1997).

_____. "Emptying the East." *Middle East International*, no. 557 (29 August 1997).

_____. "Why The KDP?" *Kurdistan Report*, no. 24 (November-December 1996):23.

O'Shea, Maria T. "Between the Map and the Reality. Some Funtamental Myths of Kurdish Nationalism." *Peuples Méditerranéens*, nos. 68-69 (1994):143-64.

_____. "The Question of Kurdistan and Iran's International Borders," in Keith McLachlan, ed. *The Boundaries of Modern Iran*, 47-56. New York: St. Martin's Press, 1994.

Pahlavan, Tschanguiz, H., "Turkish-Iranian Relations: An Iranian View," in Henri J. Barkey, ed. *Reluctant Neighbor: Turkey's Role in the Middle East*, 71-92. Washington, D.C.: United States Insitutue of Peace Press, 1996.

Pelletiere, Stephen C., Douglas V. Johnson II and Leif R. Rosenberer. *Iraqi Power and U.S. Security in the Middle East*. Carlisle Barracks: U.S. Army War College, 1990.

_____ and Douglas V. Johnson II. *Lessons Learned: The Iran-Iraq War*. Carlisle Barracks: U.S. Army War College, 1991.

_____. *The Kurds: An Unstable Element in the Gulf*. Boulder: Westview Press, 1984.

Pope, Hugh. "Conflict Over Killing." *Middle East International*, no. 444 (19 February 1993).

_____. "Pointing Fingers at Iran." *Middle East International*, no. 443 (5 February 1993).

Rahnema, Saeed and Sohrab Behded. eds. *Iran After the Revolution*. London: I. B. Tauris, 1996.

Ramazani, Rouhollah K. *The Foreign Policy of Iran: A Developing Nation in World Affairs*. Charlottesville: University of Virgina, 1966.

Randal, Johathan C. *After Such Knowledge, What Forgiveness? My Encounter with Kurdistan*. New York: Farrar, Straus and Giroux, 1997.

Robins, Philip. *Turkey and the Middle East*. New York: Council on Foreign Relations Press, 1991.

_____. "Iraq in the Gulf War: Objectives, Strategies and Problems," in Hanns W. Maull and Otto Pick, eds. *The Gulf War: Regional and International Dimensions*, 45-58. New York: St. Martiin's Press, 1989.

_____. "The Overlord State: Turkish Policy and the Kurdish Issue." *International Affairs*, no. 69, no. 4 (1993):657-76.

_____."Between Sentiment and Self-Interest: Turkey's Policy toward Azerbaijan and the Central Asian States." *Middle East Journal*, vol. 47, no. 4 (1993):593-609.

_____. "More Apparent than Real: The Impact of the Kurdish Issue on Euro-Turkish Relations," in Robert Olson, ed. *The Kurdish Nationalist Movement in the 1990s: Its Impact on Turkey and the Middle East*, 114-32. Lexington: University Press of Kentucky, 1996.

_____. "Avoiding the Question," in Henri J. Barkey, ed. *Reluctant Neighbor: Turkey's Role in the Middle East*,179-203.Washington, D.C.: United States Institute of Peace Press, 1996.

Rouleau, Eric. "Turkey: Beyond Ataturk." *Foreign Policy*, no. 103 (Summer 1996): 70-87.

Sakallıoğlu, Ümit. "Liberalism, Democracy and the Turkish Centre-Right: The Identity Crisis of the True Path Party." *Middle East Studies*, vol. 32, no. 2 (1996):142-61.

Sayarı, Sabrı. "Turkey and the Middle East." *Journal of Palestine Studies*, vol. 26, no. 3 (1997):44-55.

Şimşir, Bilâl. *İngiliz Belgeleriyle Türkiye'de "Kürt Sorunu" (1924-1938): Şeyh Sait, Ağrı ve Dersim Ayaklanmaları*. Ankara: Türk Tarih Kurumu Basım Evi, 1991.

Soğuk, Nevzat. "A Study of the Historico Cultural Reasons for Turkey's 'Inclusive Democracy." *New Political Science*, no. 26 (1993):89-116.

Tapper, Richard, ed. *Islam in Modern Turkey: Religion, Politics and Literature in a Secular State*. London: I. B. Tauris, 1991.

Thompson, Peter L. "United States-Turkey Military Relations: Treaties and Implications." *International Journal of Kurdish Studies*, vol. 9, nos. 1 & 2 (1996):103-113.

Tucker, Ernest. "The Peace Negotiations of 1736: A Conceptual Turning Point in Ottoman-Persian Relations." *The Turkish Studies Bulletin*, vol. 20, no. 1 (1996):16-37.

Tunçay, Mete. *Türkiye'de Cumhuriyeti'nde Tek Parti Yönetimi'nin Kurulması*. Ankara: Ankara: Yurt Yayınları, 1981.

Vali, Abbas. *Pre-Capitalist Iran: A Theoretical History*. New York: New

York University Press, 1993.

_____. "The Making of Kurdish Identity in Iran." *Critique*, no. 7 (1995):1-22. This is an English translation of the article listed below.

_____. "Genèse et structure du nationalisme kurde en Iran." *Peuples Méditerranéens*, nos. 18-19 (194):143-64.

Vanly, Ismet Cheriff. "The Kurds in Syria and Lebanon," in Philip G. Kreyenbroek and Stefan Sperl, eds. *The Kurds: A Contemporary Overview*, 143-70. London: Routledge, 1992.

_____. "The Kurds in the Soviet Union," in Philip G. Kreyenbroek and Stefan Sperl, eds. *The Kurds: A Contemporary Overview*, 193-218. London: Routledge, 1992.

Yalçın-Heckmann, Lale. "Ethnic Islam and Nationalism among the Kurds." Frankfurt am Main: Peter Lang, 1991.

Yaman Nesime. *"Gap": Güney Doğu Projesi: Kürdistan'da Soyyo-Ekonomik ve Siyasal Etkileri*. İstanbul: Komal Basım, 1996.

Yassin, Borhanedin, A. *Vision or Reality? The Kurds in the Policy of the Great Powers, 1941-1947*. Lund (Sweden): Lund University Press, 1995.

Yeğen, Mesut. "The Turkish State Discourse and the Exclusion of Kurdish Idenity." *Middle East Studies*, vol. 32, no. 2 (1996):216-29.

Yeşilada, Birol A. "Turkish Foreign Policy Toward the Middle East," in Atila Eralp, Müharren Tünay and Birol Yeşilada, eds., *The Political and Socioeconomic Transformation of Turkey*:169-92. Westport, CT: Praeger, 1993.

Zürcher, Erik Jan. *Opposition in the Early Turkish Republic: The Progressive Republican Party: 1924-1925*. Leiden: E. J. Brill, 1991.

_____. *Turkey: A Modern History*. London: I. B. Tauris, 1993.

INDEX

104 *Index*

Omni-balancing, international relations theory and its applicability toTurkish-Iranian foreign policy and the Kurdish question, 11-14, 16, 29, 85-6
Operation Provide Comfort (OPC), 40, 54
Ottoman empire, Kurds position in, 14, 20

Öymen, Önür (Turkish foreign ministry undersecretary), 45, 58, 71
Öcalan, Abdullah (leader of PKK), 29, 37, 46-7, 62, 66; his disagreement with Ma'sud Barzani, 46
Özsancak, Ufuk (Turkish consul in Urmiya), 57

Patriotic Union of Kurdistan (PUK), 27, 30, 37-8, 45-47, 53-6, 81
PKK (Partia Karkaren Kurdistan), 6-7, 24, 27, 29-31, 34-38, 41-55, 59-64, 66-7, 69-74, 76, 79, 81, 83; signing of "Principles of Solidarity" with KDP

Qader, Aziz (leader of Turkmen of northern Iraq), 46
Qajar empire, 3, 15-16, 36; position of Kurds in, 20-1, 74, 85
Qassemlou, Abdulrahman (leader of the KDPI-Kurdistan Democratic Party of Iran), assassination of, 49

Rafsanjani, Hashemi Hojjatolislam, (President of Iran, 1989-1997), 31, 42-3, 45, 49-50, 55, 61, 64, 67, 71, 79
Reza Shah of Iran, 21, 23
Rouhaim, Hassan, 64
Robins, Philip, 62
Rushdie, Salman, 49, 65, 68

Rashid, Mohammad Reza (Iranian consul-general in Istanbul); his expulsion from Turkey (1997), 57

Sadaabad Pact (Treaty of Non-Aggression), signing of in 1937, 24; articles of dealing with Kurdish nationalism, 24
Safavid empire, 14, position of Kurds in, 20
Sağlam, Mehmet (Turkish minister of education), 52
Satanic Verses, 49, 65-6
Sharifian policy and Arab nationalism, 5-7, 25
Shafi'i, Ali Asghar, 65
Sharafkandi, Sadegh, assassination of, 67
Shaykh Taha (Kurdish leader), 6
Shaykh, Mahmud (Kurdish leader), 6
Shaykh Ubaydallah (Kurdish leader); his Kurdish movement, 20-1; creation of Kurdish League, 21
Shaykh 'Uthman (leader of Islamic Movement of Kurdistan (IMK), 27; relations with Necmettin Erbakan, 53
Sheikh, Said, (rebellion of), 22-4, 73; affects on Islamist movements, 26; rebellion of and origins of Kurdish nationalism, 17; İsmet İnönü's description of, 18; Iran's attitude toward, 22
Shi'i(s), 4, 5, 7, 9, 40, 46, 54, 75-6
Simko Agha, 6, results of his rebellions, 21-2, assassination by Iranians, 23
Sinjan, affair of, 56-9, 65-6
Sunni(s), 4, 5, 7-9, 15, 65, 75-6
Supreme Assembly for the Islamic Revolution (SAIRI), 46
Syria, 3, 4, 6, 9, 29-30, 36-7, 51-2, 59-60, 70-1, 73, 77, 81-2, 84; definition of its foreign policy, 12-14;

---

participation in security protocols with Turkey and Iran, 41-4; relations with Iran, 61-4; role as a middle level regions power in the Middle East, 12

TAF (Turkish Armed Forces), 34, 36, 44, 46-8, 50-1, 53, 57, 61, 65-7, 69-74; attitude toward Kurdish nationalism, 26-7; their role in the politics of Turkey (1980-3), 29

Talabani, Jalal (leader of the Patriotic Union of Kurdistan (PUK), 27, 40, 45-6, 54

Tayan, Turhan (Turkish minister of defense); visit to Israel and statements while there, 60

True Path Party (TPP), 26, 43

Tripartite Security Agreements (Turkey, Iran and Syria); importance of after 1991 Gulf war, 49

Truman Doctrine, 26

Tugan, Ali (Turkish state minister), 64

Tunceli (formerly Dersim); rebellion of, 17

Turkey-Iran Frontier Treaty (1932), 15, 21, 23; definition of border and the Kurdish question, 24

Turkey, attitude toward Iraq's invasion of Iran, 28-9; attitude toward Islamic revolution in Iran, 26-36; definition of its status as a middle level power in the Middle East, 12-13; establishment of boundary with Iraq, 7, 8; importance of military agreements with Israel, 61-4; military agreements with Israel, 32-9, 77; cost of the war against the PKK, 36; energy needs of, 35-6; ethnic cleansing of Kurds, 36; GNP of, 35; incursions into northern Iraq in 1992, 1995, 1997, 30-42; Iranian capital and

investment in, 80; Islamist movement in, 50; security protocols with Iran after 1991 Gulf war, 41-4; wars against the Kurds in 1930 and 1937-8, 17; trade with Iran, 29

Turkmen, population in Iraq, 55

Turkmenistan, 33, 44, 71, 79; gas pipelines in, 34-5, 80

Urmia, 24

Vali, Abbas; characterization of Kurdish nationalism in Iran, 20-26; and objectives of the Saadabad Pact, 24-5

Veliyati, Akbar (Iranian foreign minister), 66

Weizman, Izer (President of Israel), 60

Welfare Party (WP), toppling of by TAF, 26, 72-6

Yıldız, Bekir (mayor of town of Sinjan), 56-7

Yılmaz, Mesut (Turkish prime minister and leader of the Motherland Party (MP), 57, 70-1, 84

Young Turks, 16

Zare, Said (Iranian consul in Erzurum); criticism of General Çevik Bir's statements while in Washington, D.C., 57; expulsion from Turkey in 1997, 57

Zuhab (Zohab), Treaty of signed in 1639, 15, 75; also see Kasr-i Shirin

About the Author

Robert Olson is the leading international authority on the history and politics of the Kurds. He is also a leading expert on how the nationalist movements of the Kurds have affected the foreign policies of Iraq, Turkey, Iran and Syria and these countries relations with Israel. He is currently specializing on how the growth of Kurdish nationalism after the Persian Gulf war in 1991 has impacted the politics of the Middle East, the peace process between Israel and the Arabs and the United States' foreign policies toward the region. Professor Olson is the author of *The Siege of Mosul and Ottoman Persian Relations, 1781-1747: A Study of Rebellion in the Capital and War in the Provinces of the Ottoman Empire; The Ba'th and Syria: From the French Mandate to the Era of Hafiz al-Asad; The Emergence of Kurdish Nationalism and the Sheikh Said Rebellion, 1880-1925; Imperial Meanderings and Republican By-Ways: Essays on Eighteenth Century Ottoman and Twentieth Century History of Turkey.* He is the editor of *The Kurdish Nationalist Movement in the 1990s: Its Impact on Turkey and the Middle East; Islamic and Middle Eastern Societies* and co-editor of *Iran: Essays on a Revolution in the Making; Orientalism, Islam and Islamists.* Three of Professor Olson's books have been translated into Arabic and Turkish. Some of Olson's latest articles dealing with the geopolitical and geostrategical aspects of the Kurdish question are: "The Kurdish Question in the Aftermath of the Gulf War: Geopolitic and Geostrategic Changes in the Middle East," *Third World Quarterly*, vol. 13, no. 3 (1992);475-99: "The Kurdish Question and the Geopolitic and Geostrategic Changes in the Middle East after the Gulf War, *Journal of South Asian and Middle Eastern Studies*, vol. 17, no. 4 (1994):60-83; "The Kurdish Question Four Years on: The Policies of Turkey, Syria, Iran and Iraq," *Middle East Policy*, vol 3, no. 3 (1994):136-44; "The Kurdish Question and the Kurdish Problem: Some Geopolitic and Geostrategic Comparisons," *Peuples Méditerranéens*, nos. 68-69 (1994):215-42; "The Kurdish Question and Turkey's Foreign Policy, 1991-95: From the Gulf War to the Incursion into Iraq," *Journal of South Asian and Middle Eastern Studies*, vol. 19, no. 4 (1995):1-30; "The Kurdish Question and Chechnya: Turkish and Russian Foreign Polices since the Gulf War," *Middle East Policy*, vol. 4, no. 3 (1996):106-18; "The Kurdish Question and Turkey's Foreign Policy

Toward Syria, Iran, Russia and Iraq since the Gulf War," in Robert Olson, ed. *The Kurdish Nationalist Movement in the 1990s: Its Impact on Turkey and the Middle East*, 84-113; "Iraq, Turkey and Syria Relations since the Gulf War: Kurds and Water," *Middle East Policy*, vol. 8, no. 2 (1997): 168-93.